READY FOR COLLEGE

MICHAEL
FRANCIS
PENNOCK

READY FOR COLLEGE

- DOING LAUNDRY
- WRITING PAPERS
- KEEPING YOUR FAITH
- PASSING EXAMS
- AVOIDING ALCOHOL
- MAKING FRIENDS
- MANAGING TIME
- GOING ON DATES
- EATING HEALTHY
- STAYING SAFE

AVE MARIA PRESS Notre Dame, Indiana 46556

Michael Francis Pennock is a theology teacher at St. Ignatius High School in Cleveland. He is author of several books for teenagers and adults, including the *Friendship in the Lord* series, *What We Really Want to Know*, and *This Is Our Faith*. He and his wife Carol have four children, Scott, Jennifer, Amy, and Christopher. They live in North Olmsted, Ohio.

Scripture quotations used in this text, unless otherwise noted, are taken from THE NEW JERUSALEM BIBLE, copyright © 1985 by Darton, Longman & Todd, Ltd. and Doubleday & Company, Inc. Used with permission of the publisher.

International Standard Book Number: 0-87793-607-2

Cover and text design by Elizabeth Jean French

Photography: Jim Whitmer Photography 60, 84; Bill Wittman 12, 38, 106.

Comic art by Paul Prokop

Printed and bound in the United States of America.

Library of Congress Cataloging-in-Publication Data

Pennock, Michael.

     Ready for college: doing laundry, writing papers, keeping your faith, passing exams, avoiding alcohol, making friends, managing time, going on dates, eating healthy, staying safe/by Michael Francis Pennock.

     p.   cm.

     Includes bibliographical references (p. 128).

     ISBN 0-87793-607-2

     1. College student orientation—United States. 2. College students—Religious life—United States. I. Title.

     LB2343.32.P45   1997

     378.1'98—dc21   96-40426

                                               CIP

Acknowledgements

I wish to thank the hundreds of former students who have written me from college over the years. Their trust in my advice has given me the confidence to write this book.

My heartfelt gratitude goes out in a special way to my daughter, Amy, and my wife, Carol, whose contributions and suggestions were invaluable. Amy shared her freshman experience and that of her friends (most notably, Lisa Watson and Therese Schindler) as I was writing this book. She also served as my research assistant on this book the summer before she took off to college.

Thanks, too, to former students, Lou Garcia and Brian Tomcik. They generously reported the ups and downs of their first months away at college.

I also wish to acknowledge the contributions of my friend and colleague, Paul Prokop, for his artwork. He is a fantastic teacher, Christian father and husband, and outstanding witness to the faith. I also wish to thank Fr. Bob Welsh, S.J., President of St. Ignatius High School, who originally suggested that I write this book. He has encouraged me in many of my writing projects and I am greatly indebted to him.

Finally, I wish to acknowledge the outstanding contributions of my editor, Mike Amodei. His gentle manner and enthusiastic support have inspired and encouraged me.

I am truly blessed and wish to thank the Lord and pray that this book will help its readers survive the first year of college.

Contents

Introduction
A SNAIL'S TALE

Spring had just begun. The wind still had a nip to it, and the trees were just beginning to bud. A snail began a long, arduous climb up a cherry tree. Some red-breasted robins in a nearby nest tweeted their ridicule. "You stupid snail," chirped one of them. "Where are you headed?" "Yes," chimed in the others. "Why are you climbing that tree? It doesn't have any cherries."

Ignoring their criticisms, the snail replied simply, "Don't worry. The tree will be loaded with them by the time I get there."

Perhaps the snail image doesn't particularly grab you right now. In fact, as a recent high school graduate, you might not feel like doing anything slow-moving. Likely you identify more with young birds—ready to test their wings—as you look to the new-found freedom of college life.

But truthfully, when you think about the years of college ahead of you, you might agree that the snail image is apt. You're anxious to get started on your trek, but there are questions and issues about college that seem overwhelming. You may ask yourself: Will I ever decide on a major, let alone a career? Can I keep up the grades? How will I ever handle the pressures of drinking and partying? Will I meet new friends? How can I keep up my relationships with my old friends? With my parents and siblings? With God?

But think back. Didn't you face the same kinds of hard questions as a *high school* freshman? And here you are asking yourself, "Where did the last four years go?"

Ready for College is your companion for the first part of your college journey. It's meant as a help as you prepare to go to college and for the first months of college life. *Ready for College* has grown from my own experiences as a college student, as a father of four children (two college grads, plus my college freshman daughter, and a son yet to finish high school), and as a sometimes-college teacher. Its main inspiration, however, comes from the nearly 8,000 college-bound students I have taught over the past twenty-eight years. Once in college many of these students have written or phoned me or stopped by to visit to share their experiences, cry on my shoulder, celebrate their victories, dream their dreams, or simply ask for my advice.

As a father who deeply loves his own children and as a lifelong friend to my students, I always wished I could give them a handbook of some kind to help them through their first months of college—always the toughest, to be sure. The week before my senior theology students graduate from high school, I typically share with them some of the key points you will find in this book. My students reassure me that my remarks are helpful and only wish we had more time for talking over these issues. This book provides a permanent record of our classroom discussions for all college-bound students.

Ready for College is a compendium of practical ideas and helpful hints as you begin college. It is meant to help you with all facets of the college experience: everything from how to escape the loud music in your dorm to how to defend your religious faith before your professors.

As you go off to college, my prayers and blessings are with you.

One
COUNTING DOWN THE DAYS

Your minds, then, must be sober
and ready for action.

—1 Peter 1:13

About to start college? Congratulations. Now is a good time to think of all the reasons why you want a college education. Your purpose for doing something can be a powerful motivator to keep you on course. And if your reasons match the aims of higher education, undoubtedly you will be more likely to succeed.

Kenneth L. Woodward, a senior writer for *Newsweek* magazine, believes there are three related questions an undergraduate education should force you to face:

- ▸ What is worth doing?

- ▸ What would I like to do?

- ▸ What can I do, given my limitations?[1]

How do you answer these questions? Are you trying to find out what is worth doing, that is, what is the "good life," as the philosopher Plato asked? Do you already know what you want to do, or are you like most entering freshman who classify themselves as "undecideds?" And, what are you good at? Have you *really* discovered all your potential, or do you need more challenges to teach you about your untapped gifts?

Ideally, you are going to college for lofty motives like those defined by your answers to the three questions above. But in reality, many people go to college for various other reasons: because their parents expect it of them, for job training, to prepare for a high-paying career, to meet new people (including a future spouse), to learn independence, to be with their friends, to party.

Now is the time to pause and take stock. Why are you going to college? What really is your motivation? Here is a short list of possible reasons. How many apply to you? Be honest in your assessment.

I am going to college to . . .

- have fun
- find out more about myself
- prepare for a career
- prepare for life
- keep my parents happy
- make new friends
- find a spouse
- learn how to make money

- look good in the eyes of others
- improve my Christian faith
- be with my old friends
- learn how to learn
- become a contributing member of society
- get away from home
- reach my potential
- _____

Most people have mixed motives for whatever they do. That's fine. However, one thing you will likely find out is that college is much more work than high school. You will only find the work to be worthwhile if you have some solid reasons for doing it. Having a worthwhile purpose for going to college will see you through the difficult times.

Will I Succeed?

> Success is a journey, not a destination.
> —Anonymous

How did people react to you when you first told them you planned to go to college? Perhaps your guidance counselor said, "You better improve your GPA."

Then, when you *did* get accepted into a good college, maybe a negative-thinking teacher remarked, "Just wait. It's not going to be as easy as you think."

Or possibly a cynical classmate said: "How did you ever make it? You must have an uncle in the registrar's office!"

Even your own mom or dad may have opined: "College is hard. Don't expect to do as well as you did in high school."

Every new college student I've ever known has had a lingering doubt whether or not he or she will make it through the freshman year. For example, I met a former outstanding student of mine one month before he began his freshman year at the University of Notre Dame. He said he was excited about going, but he was a bit jittery about whether or not he could cut it. Time proved that he has been able to "cut it," and so too will you. To do so, keep some basic affirmations in mind, the foremost of those being: YOU WILL SUCCEED.

To be honest, this is more fact than simply wishful thinking. A friend of mine is the director of admissions at a prestigious Jesuit college. A couple of years ago, I petitioned him to accept a student of mine. In our discussion about whether my student would be successful or not, he said that colleges today accept *only* those students who have the academic credentials and study habits to master their programs. If a student flunks out, it doesn't reflect well on the admissions department or the college in general.

The mere fact that your college accepted you is a strong vote of confidence that you will succeed. You will fit in, adjust to the new environment, make friends, and handle the work. The college believes in you. So there is no reason not to believe in yourself as well. If you make up your mind to give college your best effort from the start, within the first month of the first semester you will know that you can manage the program.

But, what is success? Before leaving this topic, think about what it means for you to be successful in college. Success, like happiness, is elusive. The more you chase it, the more it seems just out of your grasp. Instead, think of success as a by-product of your own inner vision and hard work.

One truth is clear: don't allow anyone else to define success for you. A common ploy is for others to get you to measure up to their concepts of success. In the popular media, for example, a "successful" person is anyone who is filthy rich, drop-dead gorgeous, socially powerful, or athletically superior. If you believe in these labels, and then don't achieve them, you may look at yourself as a failure. But note: How other people or society in general defines success may not be right for you, or for anyone else for that matter.

Besides, if you use society's definition for success, then even Jesus was not successful. He certainly wasn't rich, materially well-off, or powerful. He wasn't even very good at keeping friends. Look at what his friends did once he was arrested. They fled, and one, his best friend Peter, even denied knowing him.

On the other hand, spiritual writer Anthony DeMello states that success comes when we "wake up." Waking up means accepting ourselves for who we are as God's beautiful child. We don't try to live up to someone else's expectations or labels. We don't have to apologize to anyone, explain anything to anyone, or care what anyone things about us.[2]

Reject labels others put on you. Your job, clothes, hobbies, athletic skills, friends, or GPA are not you. Rather, you are God's unique creation. Reject comparing yourself to others—their looks, brains, behavior and accomplishments. Set your own standards in line with your family's standards and the standards of Christian teachings, and measure yourself only against those.

In *Happiness Is an Inside Job*, John Powell writes that happiness, or success, is something within the human heart and not something external; an "inside job" if you will. He writes that we cannot directly pursue success because it is a byproduct of living a good, wholesome, involved life.

Powell lists ten practices that he believes we must do to be successful, restated below with a further reflection or two that I believe will be of great help to you in your first months in college. By the way, *Happiness Is an Inside Job* would make excellent reading before going off to college. The ten practices are:

▼ ▼ ▼ ▼ ▼

1. **Accept yourself as you are**. Accept your strengths and weaknesses in all areas.

2. **Accept full responsibility for your life**. Do you believe that it is in your power to succeed in college? Blaming others or external factors is usually pointless.

3. **Fulfill your needs for relaxation, exercise, and nourishment**. Chapter 5 offers some practical ways to do this.

4. **Make your life an act of love**. Are you committed to loving other people in a Christian sense? Do you love yourself in a healthy way? How do you show your love for God?

5. **Stretch out your comfort zone.** The start of college is an excellent time to try something new and challenging.

6. **Learn to be a good-finder.** Good-finders are those who look for good in themselves, others, and all situations in life. Are you a good-finder? Can you find something good even in your setbacks?

7. **Seek growth, not perfection.** Very few people can achieve perfect grades. But you can aim high. And if you don't achieve your goal, you will grow for having tried.

8. **Learn to communicate effectively.** Sharing your thoughts and feelings with others, as well as listening, will help you make and keep friends. Chapter 2 discusses more about ways to communicate effectively.

9. **Learn to enjoy the good things in life.** What hobby or activity really brings you enjoyment? Can you continue to keep it up in college? Will you?

10. **Make prayer a part of your daily life.** Prayer will help you be a successful college student (see chapter 5). It will calm you, assure you of God's love and acceptance of you (despite personal setbacks), inspire and energize you, and help you keep everything in perspective. It's okay to pray for success.

▲ ▲ ▲ ▲ ▲

Review and practice these suggestions before you start college. They will go a long way to help you be a successful, happy, self-directed, loving person . . . and a good student!

Goal-Setting

Shoot at nothin, an' you'll be sure to hit it.

—An old farmer

Goal-setting and success in college go hand-in-hand. Likely you are already a goal-oriented person or you wouldn't be on your way to college. Setting goals for your freshman year is a worthwhile task and something you should do before the start of the term. Here are four goal-setting tips:

1. *Set specific goals.* For example, say "I wish to graduate from college with honors," rather than "I wish to do well." Then, ask yourself what you concretely propose to do to achieve this goal. What are specific steps you can take during your freshman year to achieve that goal?

2. *Don't be a slave to your goals.* Life is full of surprises. Someone once said, "If you want to make God laugh, just tell him your plans." God might change your schedule when you least expect it. This is exactly what happened to me in college. My plan was to be a civil-rights lawyer. But through many twists and turns, setbacks and advances, I became a religion teacher and author. Think of your goals more as *guidelines* that inspire you to action. And always be prepared in case God has other plans for your life.

3. *Set goals for the near future, not years down the line.* Goals are most helpful when they discipline you for doing today's tasks. It's okay to set your sights on med school, but be sure to set as an initial goal that of getting an "A" in the required pre-med freshman biology course. In addition, to achieve an "A" grade might mean setting the additional goal of studying an extra hour every Saturday afternoon. And possibly Sunday afternoon too!

4. *Set your own goals.* College is a time for you to grow in your individuality. It is your life to live as a responsible, loving person. Part of this process means setting your own goals and working to attain them.

Herbert Bayard Swope maintains, "I can't give you a sure-fire formula for success, but I can give you a formula for failure: try to please everyone all the time." Capable people are *self*-determining. They do what *they* think is right. They set their own goals. Psychologist Fritz Perls adds, "I did not come into this world to live up to your expectations. And you did not come into the world to live up to mine." By the way, one week before I graduated from high school a teacher of mine told me not to expect to do as well in college as I had in high school. I took his comments as a personal challenge and made it my goal to do better in college. I actually did do better—by graduating from college at the top of my class!

The Summer Before

Honor your father and your mother
so that you may live long in the land
that Yahweh your God is giving you.
—Exodus 20:12

The two or three months before college can be a stormy time, and I don't mean rain! Your relationship with your parents is changing, and it's important to proceed carefully in dealing with your mom and dad. Take heed of the following issues

You and the 3 I's

You are moving from adolescence to young adulthood. In psychological terms, this transitional period is a time of searching for *identity, independence,* and *intimacy*. You want to discover for yourself questions of identity—who you are separate from your family, school, church, friends. You are anxious to begin a more independent life where you decide for yourself and set your own agenda. You want to deepen your friendships with others who love you for who you are. Of themselves, these are worthwhile needs. However, most older adolescents making this transition want them to happen now, and not a moment later. Problems arise when these needs conflict with your parents' authority and rules.

Mom and Dad: Letting Go Is Tough

Seeing their children off to college is stressful for most parents. Intellectually, they know you have grown up and it is time for you to separate and assert your independence. They really do want you to be self-confident and self-reliant. But emotionally, when they look at you they still see the curly-haired, freckle-faced two-year-old sweetheart or that towheaded, gap-toothed, knee-bandaged five-year-old they sent off to kindergarten. Listen sometime to the lyrics of "Sunrise, Sunset" from the musical *Fiddler on the Roof*. Then you'll begin to understand the longing your parents have for you and their plaintive lament of your growing up too fast.

When you put together your need to make the future happen now with your parents' nostalgia for the past, there is bound to be a certain amount of friction at home in the summer before college. Some recent high-school graduates suddenly want all the freedom they will have once at college: no curfews, no rules, no reporting about their whereabouts. Parents, on the other hand, are ambivalent about letting go. They know that when their child leaves for college they'll be losing control. So they sometimes begin to micro-manage the lives of their son or daughter in often unrealistic ways. New rules come out of nowhere. Overreaction to slight offenses seem a daily occurrence. Fights about trivial little things pop up.

A bit of advice: Be patient with your parents and with yourself. St. Paul was right when he listed patience as the first quality of love in his famous litany on love in 1 Corinthians 13:4. Try your best to conform to your parents' wishes.

A case in point: Perhaps your parents want you to come on a family vacation. This is the last thing you want to do. You have a ton of high-school graduation parties to attend, you need to work the maximum hours to increase your summer earnings, and you really don't want to spend time traipsing around with your younger siblings. But from your parents' point of view, this may be the last time the whole family will be together. They want to hold on to and savor the family unity they have worked so hard to achieve. Here is a case where a good choice on your part would be to "bite the bullet" and go along. Who knows, you may be a bit nostalgic for family times yourself. And, you might even have fun!

Understand the turmoil your folks are experiencing. Even if it seems they can't wait for you to get out of the house—especially if you've been difficult—deep down, they don't really want you to leave. Do your best to go along and keep things pleasant at home. Compromise where possible.

Surely, you'll want a good relationship with your folks when you're at college. The best way to achieve that is to leave a good relationship at home.

Talk It Out . . . Now!

> Commend what you do to Yahweh,
> and what you plan will be achieved.
> —Proverbs 16:3

A key to maintaining a good relationship with your parents is to keep the lines of communication open. Make time in the weeks before you begin college to discuss four very important topics with your folks: *values, academic expectations, communication,* and *money.* Here is some more information about each:

Values College is a time of separations, independence, thinking on your own, and becoming your own person. You will meet many people who have different values than you or your parents. They will challenge your beliefs and may even tempt you to forsake them.

Your parents know all this, and they worry. They worry about things that may not seem important to you: like whether you'll get a tattoo, get your ears pierced (if a guy), change your hair style, wear grubby clothes, forget the cleanliness habits you've learned since babyhood, and eat only junk food. They also worry about things that are very significant: that you might abandon your faith, experiment with drugs, abuse alcohol, or engage in promiscuous sex. Remember the definition of a parent: "one who worries . . . often needlessly."

Needless worry or not, your parents care deeply about you. They know that the new environment you are going into might tempt you to leave your good family values behind. Now is the time to discuss these issues honestly with your parents. Ideally, you can reassure your mom and dad that you will not do anything foolish and that you will engage in only safe and moral behavior. In turn, hopefully your parents will reassure you of their love and support during these crucial years of growth.

Academic Expectations The main reason for going to college is to learn and be educated. The knowledge you gain can help you determine interests and skills and eventually prepare you for job, career, and vocation. Doing well in college means you must go to class, study, take notes, study, read texts, study, do research, study, work through problems, study, write papers, study, take tests, and study. And for the privilege of doing all of the above you and your parents will likely pay a lot of money!

Believe it or not, college education is still a privilege, not a right. The state does not guarantee its citizens advanced education. If you want it, you have to pay for it through loans, scholarships, grants, work-study programs, jobs, and good old hard cash . . . lots of it. Most likely your parents are sacrificing significantly for you to go to college.

It is a good idea to get out in the open right before you begin college what your parents expect from you academically and how your academic performance is tied to their financial assistance.

I know parents who tell their kids, "I will not pay for D's and F's." I have told my own children, "I will help you for the equivalent of four years of college. Anything beyond that and you are on your own." I also know parents who'll stop paying once their son's or daughter's GPA falls below an "A" average. Personally, I think the first two positions are reasonable, but this last one is simply unfair. Parents must know that college is difficult enough. By setting an unrealistic GPA goal they are only adding unnecessary pressure that contributes to failure.

If you have a good relationship with your parents, it should be easy to compromise on this issue of academic expectations. However, if you think your parents' expectations are too high, try to involve other family members or friends who have had young people go through college to help you work out a solution. No matter what, assure your folks that you will always work hard and try your best. And let them know you really appreciate any sacrifices they are making on your behalf.

Communication Decide ahead of time how you plan to communicate with your parents while in college. Even if you live at home, your new schedule may differ so much from your parents' that you may need to plan times when you can be together and catch up on each other's goings on. For those living away at school, the issue is equally important.

Some parents expect a phone call at least once per week. Others are happy to get a letter every other week. Another popular option is to e-mail one another on a regular basis. My daughter discovered e-mail soon into her freshman year and corresponded with us and her friends around the country.

Most college dorms allow each room to have its own phone. My kids also had answering machines. If we wanted to contact them, we were only a message away. But we still wanted them to feel free to call whenever they wished. Phone calls are not inexpensive. You can keep your phone bills to a minimum by:

- ▸ calling your parents at a planned time.

- ▸ writing down topics you want to talk about so that you are prepared and don't waste time remembering what you wanted to say.

- ▸ calling when the rates are the cheapest: usually after 11 PM on weekdays, all day Saturday, and before 5 PM on Sundays.

Money A college student wired home this message: "In a bad way. No friends. No money. Please help!" His father sent a return wire: "Make friends!"

"Spending money" is another issue to work out before you begin college: How much you will need? How you will get it? What you will do when you run out? Like the general population, some students handle money well, others don't. My own children were proof of this. My son always ran out of money and had to borrow frequently to finish the semester. In contrast, my daughter saved enough from her college allowance to have a down payment for a car by her senior year.

For all college students, there is never *enough* money. In fact, this issue warrants a closer study. The next section examines ways you can survive financially in your freshman year.

Money, Money, Money

The lack of money is the root of all evils.
—Mark Twain

In regards to the college experience, Mark Twain's tongue-in-cheek rewriting of 1 Timothy 6:10 has some validity. There are rarely enough funds to cover all the expenses of a college education. After the tuition and room and board bills are paid, the cash outlays have just begun.

For example, you'll need textbooks. You will probably be quoted a dollar amount by your college to allocate for texts. Add two to three hundred dollars to their estimate. Depending on your major, some books cost 50 dollars or more. As a cost-saving measure, buy used books whenever possible. Be sure they are relatively unmarked, with the highlighting not overdone. A second cost-saver: Don't sell your books back to the bookstore when you have finished with them. Rather, post a notice in the student center and sell the books yourself. You'll likely get a higher price.

You'll also need money for supplies (paper, notebooks, pens, computer disks, and the like), lab fees, and car expenses. If you're living away from home, phone bills, laundry, snacks, postage stamps, and toiletries will add to your expenses.

If your home is a distance from campus, you'll need money for travel back and forth from home to school, a major expense. For commuters this involves having and maintaining a car: gas, oil, parking passes, and repairs. For residents, travel money is also a major consideration. Money-savers for getting you and your supplies to and from school include hitching rides and renting trailers or trucks with other students from your city, seeking savings on airfare through advance purchase of tickets and even the less expensive bus fares.

Remember, too, you'll need cash for dates, parties, movies, sporting events, and other forms of entertainment.

Finally, be aware of one-time hidden costs that hit freshmen especially hard: for example, a carpet, fan, desk lamp, and small refrigerator for your dorm room. Consider buying these items used. Also try to share some of these expenses with a roommate.

A key to financial survival during your freshman year is to make *budgeting* a top priority. Here are some more tips:

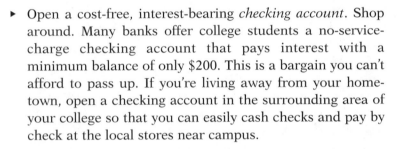

▸ Open a cost-free, interest-bearing *checking account*. Shop around. Many banks offer college students a no-service-charge checking account that pays interest with a minimum balance of only $200. This is a bargain you can't afford to pass up. If you're living away from your hometown, open a checking account in the surrounding area of your college so that you can easily cash checks and pay by check at the local stores near campus.

▸ Ask for an *automated-teller machine (ATM) card* with your checking account. Find out if there is any service charge for withdrawals. I know a student who racked up over $20 of service fees in just one month by making primarily $10 or $20 withdrawals. Make sure your bank does not charge for ATM withdrawals at your school's ATM service center.

▸ Beware! Banks will offer *credit cards* to you with all kinds of incentives to take them up on the offer. They want to hook you with a "buy now, pay later" dream, or more accurately, scheme. Credit card companies downplay their usurious twenty percent interest rates on unpaid balances. Furthermore, they know if you run the card up to its maximum amount and you can't pay, your parents will more than likely bail you out to save you future credit woes.

▸ Should you get a credit card or not? On the plus side, credit cards are convenient, safe, easily replaced if stolen, and good when traveling or for emergencies. Furthermore, credit card companies usually back up the purchaser in a dispute with a vendor. Credit cards also help you cash checks, get cash through an ATM, and help establish a credit history.

An estimated sixty percent of today's college students have credit cards. However, before signing up for one, be sure to discuss it with your parents. They'll have some good insights about how to handle credit. And they may instead suggest a debit card. A *debit* card allows your parents to deposit funds into a checking account, which you can access while on campus. Bank statements go to your parents who can then help track expenditures.

Also, balance the positive reasons for having a credit card against the tendency to use credit cards for impulse buying. One estimate holds that people with credit cards spend about one-third more than they would if they didn't have one. Wise stewards only buy what they can pay for. And as a prudent college student, you should always discuss large purchases with your parents.

▲ ▲ ▲ ▲ ▲

By way of summary, unless your family has recently hit a big lottery prize, you must learn to *budget* your money. Now is a good time to work with your parents to come up with a realistic budget for your first semester. Use the following chart to plan:

Monthly Allocation							
travel							
texts							
supplies							
local transportation							
phone							
clothing							
laundry							
toiletries							
snack food							
recreation							
emergencies/misc.							
total monthly expenses							

What do you think? Is this a realistic figure? Verify each item with at least three college sophomores you know. Ask them to name any unanticipated expenses that cropped up during their freshman year. Revise your estimated budget accordingly. Then plan to stick to it.

Freshmen Orientation

Perhaps the most valuable result of all education is
the ability to make yourself do the thing you have to
do when it has to be done, whether you like it or not.

—Aldous Huxley

Colleges vary on how they handle freshmen orientation. Some colleges hold a grand orientation weekend for all freshmen (and sometimes their parents, too) before the term begins. During this weekend, registration for fall courses may also be handled. Other colleges have groups of freshmen come in throughout the summer for orientation and registration. Still others handle course selection by mail with orientation taking place at another time. Orientations can be intense days of meetings and tours, or week-long extravaganzas with socials and icebreakers. Some orientations are handled intermittently over the first semester.

Regardless of when orientation takes place, if you have a choice, *register for courses as early as possible*. Also, keep in mind the following tips when registering for your first semester:

▸ Ask around among upper class students about the professors of the courses you are considering. What is required of a particular course? How does the professor rate as a lecturer? When in doubt, it is always better to choose recommended profs over courses that "seem" appealing.

▸ Don't overload with units your first semester in college. Fifteen or 16 hours are plenty. You need to prove that you can succeed. Balance your choices between reading intensive courses (like history) and math and science courses, if possible.

▸ Most colleges require a core of basic courses for all undergrads, regardless of major. Other courses or prerequisites you may have to take depend on your high-school program, SAT or ACT scores, or placement exams.

The core typically consists of one or two English courses, math, natural science (biology, earth science, chemistry, physics), social science (history, psychology, sociology, government), physical education, and sometimes a foreign language or computer course.

Sign up for mostly core courses your first semester. Sample a variety of subject areas. You might choose one tough course, one easy course, and a couple of moderately difficult ones. They will serve as a foundation on which to build, especially if you have yet to choose a major. *Suggestion*: If a particular core area is one you do not like or have had a tough time with in high school, don't take a course in that area your first semester. You need a successful freshman year. By waiting, you'll have time to get more information about an ideal prof in order to get you through the "dreaded" requirement.

- Decide if you learn best in the morning or afternoon. This is not an automatic decision. Even though you may believe you would learn better later in the day, studies have proven that people retain knowledge best in morning hours. Besides, coming from high school, you are used to being in class in the morning.

  However, true night owls should probably not sign up for 8 am classes. Pick your courses accordingly. You might even consider taking an evening course that meets for three hours once a week. This will free some study time during the day.

- Choose a schedule that eliminates "down time." Better to have three courses in the morning than one at 8 am, another at noon, and another at 4 pm. The all-too-human tendency with a schedule like that would be to waste time waiting around for class.

Either during summer orientation or through the mail, the student-life office will ask you about roommate preferences. Be honest in what you report about your likes and dislikes. It might save later problems. For example, if second-hand smoke drives you crazy, you should make sure to indicate a preference for a non-smoking roommate, even if smoking is not allowed in the dorm.

Also, if your college does offer a summer orientation program, use the opportunity to meet new people there. A good icebreaker is to introduce yourself and tell where you are from. Then take it from there.

Finally, your orientation days are a good time to get to know the campus and where some of your classes might be. A legible campus map is also a good thing to keep with you.

What to Take for the Dorm

All the possessions of mortals are mortal.
—Metrodorus

Packing for dorm-living will probably be the toughest job you will face in the days before you leave for college. You must strike a balance between transporting everything you own to bare-bones packing that leaves you needing everything once you get to school. The following lists provide for essentials. Fill in other items based on your gender and special needs:

Clothing

- ✔ underclothing
- ✔ jacket, gloves, hat, scarf, boots
- ✔ shoes (casual and dress)
- ✔ athletic shoes
- ✔ sweaters

- ✔ casual clothes (for class)
- ✔ sleeping clothes (pajamas, sweats, etc.)
- ✔ dress shoes (for interviews, formal social functions)
- ✔ rain gear
- ✔ sport's gear and clothing

Hint: Print your name on your clothing in an indelible laundry marker

Personal Items

- ✔ shampoo, conditioner, comb, brush, hair dryer
- ✔ medicines, vitamins
- ✔ extra clothes hangers
- ✔ laundry bag, detergents, fabric softener
- ✔ big bath towels, washcloths
- ✔ bed sheets, mattress pad, pillow cases

- ✔ toothpaste, toothbrush, floss
- ✔ first aid supplies
- ✔ wastebasket
- ✔ soap, deodorant, other toiletries
- ✔ nail clipper
- ✔ thongs to wear in the shower

Room Items

- ✔ CD player
- ✔ coffee mug
- ✔ inexpensive camera
- ✔ refrigerator
  (check with roommate)
- ✔ phone and answering
  machine (check with
  roommate)
- ✔ calculator
- ✔ extension cord
- ✔ foot locker

- ✔ desk supplies: paper, pens,
  highlight markers, ruler,
  white-out, scissors, tape,
  stapler, notebook

- ✔ Walkman
- ✔ stationary and stamps
- ✔ travel iron
- ✔ lamps (desk, floor),
  clip-on book lights
- ✔ word processor or personal
  computer with surge
  protector
- ✔ travel alarm clock
- ✔ message board for door
- ✔ carpet
  (check with roommate)
- ✔ foot locker

- ✔ fan

For Academic Survival

- ✔ wall calendar
- ✔ thesaurus
- ✔ dictionary

- ✔ bible
- ✔ assignment book
- ✔ manual of writing style

Transportation

- ✔ bike with u-lock

The best way to transport your belongings to and from your dorm is in bundling suitcases.

If you forget something, it can be shipped to you. If it's not a life-or-death item, your parents can bring it to you their first visit to campus or you can pick it up when you return home.

By the way, *do not* bring valuable jewelry, prized possessions, or a great deal of cash. Unfortunately, college students do steal from each other. My son had an expensive mountain bike permanently "borrowed" from him. He told me he wasn't sure if he locked it or not. *A bit of fatherly advice*: "Always lock your bike."

And Another Thing:
More Questions and Suggestions

Remember, nothing is small in the eyes of God.
—St. Thérèse of Lisieux

The last section of this chapter covers some other commonly asked questions and issues raised by my students about their preparation for and first days of college life.

How do I say "good-bye" to my high-school sweetheart?

Having a serious boyfriend or girlfriend when you go off to college adds strain to an already stressful situation. I know many former students who left college within the first semester of arrival to be near their high-school sweethearts.

To be honest, most high-school relationships unravel when one or both partners go off to college. College presents opportunities to broaden oneself both intellectually and socially. Absence does not always make the heart grow fonder as college freshman discover the green pastures of many new people to date. And there is really some truth in the adage: out of sight, out of mind.

College is a time of change, both for you and the person you leave behind. At the least, you should give yourself the opportunity to date other people in college. Trying to keep an exclusive long-distance relationship going will lead to emotional struggles—including feelings of guilt—when you feel attracted to someone else.

The summer after high school is the time to discuss with your boyfriend or girlfriend the need to go to college with your options open. If your relationship back home is the "real thing," neither time nor miles will destroy it. Discuss the future honestly. But don't make any promises you can't keep.

Certainly you can keep in touch with the person you've had a serious relationship with in high school. An occasional phone call is appropriate. Letter-writing is a better way to remain connected on a deeper level. And, if possible, plan to catch up with one another in person during school breaks.

Giving your boyfriend or girlfriend room to develop is beneficial for him or her as well. Grasping too tightly to anyone stifles an individual's growth and can drive that person away.

Should I bring a car to college?

Unless you are a commuter student, you're smart if you discipline yourself and leave your car at home.

Listen to the sucking sound of money leaving your wallet for gas, insurance, maintenance and car repairs. Having a car is very costly, especially if you are on a modest budget.

Also, realize that you will immediately be Ms. or Mr. Popularity the minute your friends and acquaintances know you have a car. They will beg you ("just this once") to take them places. Good person that you are, it will be hard to turn them down. The time spent running errands for others could negatively affect your academics.

You could respond, "I can let them *use* my car." But what if they are in an accident? You share in the responsibility. And your insurance rates (or your parent's rates) will go through the roof.

It is cheaper, more convenient, and healthier to walk, use a bike, or, if available, use a campus shuttle service.

Will I be able to hold a job and keep up with studies?

During your first semester you should not take a job. Many students will have to work sometime during their college years. But try at all costs to avoid taking a job during your first semester. Your first semester involves so many changes and stresses that you need to be free to devote all your energies to coping and to becoming a top-notch student. Once you are well-versed in the academic routine of college, then you will know what it will take to get good grades and hold down a job.

Should I bring important documents like my financial aid award or leave them at home?

It's probably better to leave most important documents at home. In any case, create a file to save your important documents, including financial aid awards, tuition payment receipts, report cards, letters of recommendation, and academic transcripts. Being able to show written documentation of the highlights of your college career will often be required of you.

Include in your file a copy of the college catalog from your first year of college. Even if department requirements in your academic major are later changed, most colleges will allow you to complete your course of study and graduate under the requirements from when you first enrolled at their school.

I know college is expensive. What are some things I can do to save money?

For the frugal, there are many money-saving tips that can be implemented. Some ideas are:

- ▸ Buy your school and dorm supplies at a discount store, not at the college bookstore where prices are likely higher.

- ▸ Take advantage of the free or inexpensive entertainment (including movies and concerts) that take place on campus.

- ▸ Limit how much money you withdraw at any one time from your account, especially at ATM machines.

- ▸ Use the campus meal plan to your benefit. Don't eat out after you've already paid for the meal plan. Also, if your food service allows, carry out any food you can't eat. For example, take an extra piece of fruit to your room for a late-night snack. Trips to the candy machine can kill your budget and your waistline.

- Balance your checking account after *every* purchase. Banks charge a penalty fee (around $25) for checks returned because of insufficient funds in the account.

- If you do choose to keep a credit card, be sure to pay your balance in full every month. This will allow you to avoid the inflated interest charges.

- Ask your parents to attach an amendment to their homeowner's insurance policy that will cover your belongings from theft or damage while you live at college.

How do I do laundry?

A good question, since college students living in dorms are responsible for doing their own laundry. The best way to learn is to take a special course of instruction from your mom, dad, brother, grandmother, or aunt this summer. At the minimum, commit to memory these laundry hints:

1. Stock up on quarters. A load of wash can cost up to two dollars.

2. Don't bleach colored clothes.

3. Don't wash your colored and white clothes together (unless you want dingy pink underwear).

Two
THE FIRST WEEKS ON CAMPUS

The popular author Robert Fulghum wishes he could give a high-school graduating class a speech on what it means to be a "grownup." In it, he would ask the graduates questions like these:

- ▶ *Could you clean the sink strainer?*
- ▶ *Could you plunge out the toilet?*
- ▶ *Could you clean up babies when they poop and pee?*
- ▶ *Could you wipe runny noses?*
- ▶ *Could you clean ovens and grease traps and roasting pans?*
- ▶ *Could you carry out the garbage?*
- ▶ *Could you bury pets when they get run over in the street?*

As Fulghum points out, being an adult is lots of dirty work.[1]

Going to college is a step to adulthood, that is, independent living. Fulghum's questions raise some others related to the dirty work you will be faced with as a college student. For example:

- Could you honestly tell a roommate that certain of his or her habits are driving you crazy?
- Could you accept others who hold different beliefs and values than you?
- Could you admit you are homesick?
- Could you ask for help when you need it?
- Could you risk rejection by initiating new relationships?
- Could you commit to the requirements of a campus activity without undermining your other obligations?

In this chapter, you will uncover some of the difficulties (a.k.a. "dirty work") confronting the freshman newly arrived on campus, including how to:

- say good-bye to your parents
- get along with your roommate
- survive first-week jitters
- deal with homesickness
- make new friends
- appreciate, not reject, differences in people
- determine when and if to join in campus activities

Saying Good-bye to Mom and Dad

"Always Leave Them Laughing
When You Say Good-bye"
—a song by George M. Cohan

After a hectic few weeks packing and saying good-bye to your high-school friends, you will eventually be ready to go to college. It will be normal for you to have mixed feelings about this. On the one hand, you'll feel excitement about the new experience; on the other, you might be a bit fearful and apprehensive about letting go of the old and familiar.

Part of the blur of going away to college is saying good-bye to your parents. It is typical for newly-arrived freshmen to want their parents to leave campus as soon as they drop them off. You might even begin to drop not-so-subtle hints to your parents that maybe they should get going to beat the traffic as soon as your key turns the lock of your dorm room.

However, some freshman find it tougher to say good-bye. To delay their parents from leaving too soon, they may invent ploys to keep their parents around a little longer. They may walk with them to the college bookstore to pick up a sweat shirt. Or they might too eagerly jump at their parents' invitation to go out to dinner to a fancy restaurant, even if it means missing an orientation meeting.

Elation over new-found freedom mixed with wariness about letting go is common enough. Going away to college is likely your first real separation from your parents. Thus, ambivalence about assuming new responsibilities, fears of the unknown, and being overwhelmed by the swirl of activity on your day of arrival can make saying good-bye difficult.

And it might also be tough for your folks. They know only too well that their relationship with you will change. Some parents find this hard to take. They may be reluctant to let go, to accept that you are really leaving them. Some parents even resort to behavior that appears irrational. For example, they might insist on setting up your dorm room the way *they* like it. Or they might give last-minute lectures on topics they have already rehashed a thousand times.

Be patient with your parents and with yourself. Here are five tips on how to handle those "last good-byes" between you and your parents:

1. If he or she wants to, let your mom or dad help you make your dorm bed. This will help them feel as if they've left their personal touch on your living space.

2. Formally introduce your parents to your roommate and your resident adviser (RA). This will help you to establish the tone that accompanies a more mature parent/child relationship.

3. If possible, go to dinner with your folks if this is something they really want to do. This would be a good time to:

- ▸ Reassure them that you will call or write, weekly at first. (Make sure to follow through with your promise.)

- ▸ Invite your parents for a visit. Most colleges have a Parent's Weekend (usually six to eight weeks into the first semester). Tell them you genuinely want them (and your siblings) to be there.

4. Walk your parents to their car (or airport shuttle) when they are ready to go home. Leave your roommate and new friends back in the dorm. Share some sincere hugs and tears, but remember this isn't a death: you will see them again.

5. As you return, alone, to your dorm, say a prayer for your parents' safe return home and for your ability to live by the values they imparted to you.

Getting Along with Your Roommate

Be ready to do good at every opportunity; not to go slandering other people but to be peaceable and gentle, and always polite to people of all kinds.
—Titus 3:1-2

If you're going to live with a roommate you've never met before, you're likely to have many questions beginning with "What if my roommate. . . ?" Here are some possible variations:

- ▸ abuses alcohol or drugs?

- ▸ smokes in the room?

- ▸ wants her boyfriend (or his girlfriend) to sleep over?

- ▸ steals from me?

- ▸ is an exchange student who speaks a different language?

- is of a different race than me?

- is a slob?

- always has creepy friends hanging out in our room?

- listens to music I loathe?

- stays up all night when I'm trying to sleep?

- is gay?

Some of these questions raise real problems; others are not problems at all. A good thing to remember is that your relationship with your roommate can be positive and satisfying, even if you do not become best friends. You can have different personalities, races, interests, family backgrounds, and academic majors and still have an honest relationship built on mutual respect. Keep the following suggestions in mind for a positive roommate experience.

1. Have a positive attitude.

From the very first, expect that you *will* get along with your roommate. Greet the person warmly when you are introduced.

Keep an open mind about the person. Don't judge solely on your first impressions.

At all costs resist *stereotyping* your roommate. Prejudgments made out of ignorance or lack of experience breed fear. Give your roommate a chance. After all, a person's nationality, religion, race, geographic origin, socio-economic condition, or sexual orientation are not bases for condemnation. Your Christian faith asks you to respect everyone as a child of God. Remember: your siblings may not always be your closest friends, but you've learned to get along with them. Aim to be congenial, and 99 percent of the time you should have a positive experience with your roommate.

2. Be patient with yourself and your roommate.

It takes time to get to know another person. Give yourself a chance. As an anonymous author once wrote, "Patience is the best remedy for most trouble."

Do some activities together the first few days at college; for example, walk to class or share a meal. Talk about your likes and dislikes. Tell about your family and high-school experience. Be a good listener and allow your roommate to share about himself or herself too.

3. Ground your relationship in honest communication.

A key to any successful relationship is an exchange of honest, gut-level communication. Practice the art of genuine communication and you'll avoid most roommate problems. Within the first week, be sure to discuss the following issues:

> *Borrowing and loaning.* What can your roommate borrow from you without your permission? What personal stuff is "hands off"—clothes, supplies, toiletries (borrowing toothbrushes, for example, is really not healthy!), money, computer? To save arguments later, clearly state what you want in this regard.

> *Visiting hours.* What is the curfew for visitors? How will you handle boyfriends or girlfriends? It's best to abide by dorm regulations in this area, since both of you may be

held responsible for breaking this rule. It is perfectly okay (and morally correct) for you to say that you will not give up the room for an overnight stay of your roommate's friend of the opposite sex. You might as well share your values on this issue up front. If your roommate is gay, apply the same standards.

Sleep. Are you a night-owl? Do you need your ten hours of sleep, even if it means being in bed by nine? What will bother you (lights, music, visitors) when you are trying to fall asleep?

Quiet hours. Do you expect to study in your dorm room? What hours will you keep sacrosanct for study?

Space. How will you divide the space in your room? Some roommates prefer to make bunks or move their beds to one side of the room to create more living space.

Music. Share your music preference. Try to agree on an acceptable volume level for whatever kind of music you each like.

Phone bills. Most likely, the phone company will not send separate bills. You will have to work out a way to divide common charges and assign the long distance calls.

Cleanliness. Are you a neatness freak? Or are you on the sloppy side? How do you plan to keep your space livable? Agree on and assign cleaning chores, just as you might do within a family.

Smoking and drinking. Colleges and individual dorms have particular rules about smoking and drinking in dorm rooms. Make sure to follow them. Also, make sure to state your opinion on alcohol, tobacco, and drug use. Many college freshmen who abuse alcohol for the first time end up vomiting. Make every effort to insure this doesn't happen in your room, where the odor may linger for the rest of the term.

Confidences. Just by sharing the same space, you will learn some private details about your roommate's life. How will you handle these "secrets" you learn about each other?

Pet peeves. What really bothers you? This is your best chance to tell each other of your own idiosyncrasies and habits.

If you agree to be open and honest from your first meeting it will be much easier to gently broach a subject of concern when it arises. Resolve to deal with problems right away instead of letting them simmer. Recall your understanding of the guidelines you agreed to. Always negotiate when you can, but make sure to speak up for your rights too.

4. Always show respect.

Remember the golden rule: do to others as you would have them do to you. Being considerate and respectful of each other will go a long way to making dorm living a pleasant experience. Simple little courtesies like taking phone messages, respecting your roommate's privacy, and picking up an occasional item for the other while shopping will strengthen a roommate relationship.

5. Don't forget security issues.

Unfortunately, college students are subject to the effects of original sin like any other human being. They steal. Agree to lock your dorm room every time you leave it, even for short trips to the bathroom. If you are going out for any length of time, lock the windows too. Many a roommate relationship has gone sour when someone forgot to lock the door and the other person had something ripped off.

6. Always be willing to compromise.

Living with another person in close quarters involves give-and-take compromise. Flexibility is important. Trying to see the other's viewpoint is helpful in reaching mutual understanding.

Most times you will be able to deal with any problems that come up. But sometimes it is tough to resolve your differences. When you reach that point, you might ask your RA to mediate your dispute. Perhaps the RA can help you reach an agreement. A third party can often look at issues more objectively. In more extreme cases, you might even ask the RA to arbitrate your dispute. Arbitration involves agreeing beforehand to abide by the RA's judgment, whether it favors you or not.

In very rare cases, you might have to request a room change. Perhaps your roommate repeatedly steals your money, is a drug abuser whose behavior is affecting your academic performance, is repeatedly using the room for sexual liaisons, or refuses to compromise on any issue. It is painful to request a room change in the middle of a term, but sometimes it is the only resort. Remember you do have the *right* to a safe, supportive, and healthy living environment to pursue your education.

Surviving First Week Jitters

When the going gets tough, the tough get going.
—from a locker room wall

You may have heard of future-shock. Prepare yourself for freshman-shock! An explosion of activity confronts college freshmen the first few weeks at college. You may find some of the activities, experiences, and people scary, overwhelming, and challenging. But others may prod you to peak performance. There is no telling exactly how *you* will react to all the novelty.

First, realize that it is perfectly normal to feel uncomfortable in a new environment. Despite appearances, most freshmen also are apprehensive.

Second, convince yourself that you will survive the stress of being new to college life. Hang on for a few weeks and you will look back and have a good laugh.

Third, if you encounter any of the following situations, don't panic! Try the suggested remedies for each instead.

Hassles with Dorm Living

"Dormitory" comes from a Latin word that means "sleep." As you will soon find out if you live in a college dorm, that is a misnomer. Sleep and dorm-living hardly go hand-in-hand. Living in a dorm is a real eye-opener. Literally.

Perhaps you lucked out and got an ideal roommate (or room-mates). But this does not guarantee a spacious dorm room, some of which are about the size of broom closets. Then there is the noise! It might seem that someone on every floor is playing his or her music at full volume . . . 24 hours a day. You quickly learn that your dorm room is not the ideal place to study.

Not only will some floormates constantly party, you may even find pranksters who pull the fire alarm at 3 am, rousing every-one from sleep. Then, there is the food! College students love to complain about dorm food, and rightly so. How can it possibly measure up to home cooking?

To cope with these inconveniences of college living you should:

- Develop a sense of humor. Living in a dorm requires give-and-take, patience, and the ability to laugh.

- Invest in a Walkman, ear plugs, or even eye shades. There *are* ways to block out noise to get sleep.

- Search for a quiet and safe place on campus to study (for example, a carrel in the library or an empty class-room).

- Keep your refrigerator stocked with healthy snacks (fruit, vegetables, etc.). They are less likely to be snatched by your roommate or other floormates. And, this healthy fare will balance the great amount of delivered pizza you are bound to eat.

Loneliness

You go to a biology class with 75 other students and you don't know anyone. Or, you are the only person from your high school in your dorm and are feeling lonely and isolated. Or, you are a commuter who notices the "on-campus people" sticking together and ignoring "outsiders" like you. Unlike high school where you knew everyone, college may seem like a vast wasteland where no one knows your name. Here are some ways to overcome the occasions of loneliness that strike during the first weeks:

- Invite someone from class to meet you for lunch.

- If you commute to campus, find the main spot where the other commuters hang out and socialize. You're bound to meet a kindred spirit there.

- If you live on campus, arrange to eat dinner several times a week (at least) with your roommate.

- Talk to someone in line with you at the bookstore.

- Visit the sports complex. You're likely to find someone who is looking for a pickup basketball game, a spotter in the weight room, a handball opponent, or a companion to swim laps with in the pool.

- Buy a dozen post cards and jot a line to friends at home or on other campuses. Nothing dispels isolation like a stuffed mailbox of news from old friends.

Study Blues

It's a Thursday night, the third week of the semester. Everyone else is out partying. You are the only one swamped with homework. You begin to wonder: What's going on here?

Keep these points in mind:

- If you are studying hard, then you are doing the right thing. Remember that your main "job" right now is to study. Many freshmen learn this lesson too late. Look for many of the Thursday night partiers on the academic probation roll at the end of the semester. This *won't* happen to you.

- In fact, you should work even harder to get ahead of your work in a couple of your tougher courses. This may even mean putting in some study hours on a Friday and/or Saturday night. Then, reward yourself by breaking the routine and joining in with some of the social scene.

Demanding Profs

You are taking an introductory writing course. Included in the course requirements is a weekly essay. You receive a "D" for your first composition. You're very disappointed because the lowest grade you ever received in high school was a "B," and that was in a tough physics course. What do you do next? Consider the following:

- Don't give up. Remind yourself that college is tougher than high school.

- Give yourself time to learn and to grow. Many instructors in freshman or introductory courses assign low grades at the start of a semester. They are looking for their students to improve. And you will improve if you heed their suggestions.

- If possible, move your seat to the front of the classroom. Participate actively by asking questions and taking part in the discussion. Many profs will give you the benefit of the doubt if they know you care about their course and are trying to improve.

- Make an appointment to go see your instructor to find out in more detail how you can improve.

- Seek out a teacher's assistant (usually upper division or graduate students) for additional help.

Athletic Setbacks

You had a five handicap as captain of your high-school golf team. But when you try out for the State U. golf team, you don't make it. Possible ways to respond positively are:

- Don't sweat it. Depending on the college and the sport, competition for a position on a varsity team can be fierce. This does not so much reflect on your talent as to comment on the excellence of the program.

- Many colleges have an active intramural sport's program. Sign up to participate in at least one seasonal sport.

- Try a new activity. You'll not only expand your horizons, but you may learn to enjoy it.

Sniffles

What happens when you get sick? Toward the end of your second week on campus you wake up one morning with a sore throat and headache. Mother isn't around to dispense aspirin and her sure-cure chicken soup. Here are some alternative actions:

- Try a recommended over-the-counter medicine, including vitamins. Make sure you are eating healthy foods and a well-balanced diet. Check to see if you are sleeping in a draft. Dry your hair well before going to bed.

- If you don't improve in a day or so, visit the school clinic. You don't want to miss classes and be sapped of energy for study this early in the term.

Missing Home

Loneliness is the first thing which
God's eye named not good.
—John Milton from *Tetrachordon*

I asked a former student, a star high-school quarterback with a winning and confident personality, what was the toughest part of his freshman year in college. He replied, "Homesickness. I never realized I would miss my family and friends so much. I was always calling home the first few weeks."

Most freshmen experience homesickness, defined as "a negative emotional response to leaving home." One study revealed that almost 70 percent of freshmen were homesick at some time. On the plus side, two-thirds of these students overcame homesickness after one week.[2]

Loneliness, a lack of close friends, the stress-filled world of college, a sense of insecurity caused by disorientation in new surroundings—all of these contribute to the very *normal* feelings of homesickness.

Homesickness can be mild in those who have many high-school friends attending college with them or who live close enough to get home to visit when they need to. It is usually more severe in students who are very close to their families, have never been away for any length of time, and who attend a school that is an airplane flight away from home. The worst cases of homesickness result in students transferring schools to be nearer to home or dropping out of college.

There are several ways to survive homesickness Here are some:

- ▸ Remember that homesickness is very natural. It is a normal stage in the process of separating from home and becoming an independent, self-directed adult. The pain will pass, usually sooner rather than later.

- ▸ Don't compare yourself to others who appear to have it "together." Many freshmen probably feel like you do but hide behind smiling faces.

- Keep busy. Put your energies into your studies.

- Make a conscious effort to meet people. Introduce yourself to a couple of new people each day. Most freshmen are friendly and as eager as you to meet someone new.

- Talk things over with your RA. Resident advisors have had training in helping freshmen adjust to the new college environment.

- Stay in touch with friends and family at home. Letters and phone calls can be your lifeline as you settle into the college routine.

- Consider getting involved in an extracurricular activity. This will keep you busy and will introduce you to new people.

- Cultivate close friendships. A friend helps shatter loneliness. The next section offers some ways to do this.

- Pray. Praying will enhance your self-esteem. Praying will also reassure you of God's constant care for you, especially in your new surroundings.

Making Friends

I have called you friends. . . . It was not you
who chose me, but I who chose you.
—John 15:15-16

Forming new friendships is a highlight of going to college. Some of these new friends will remain friends throughout your life. Many men and women even meet their future spouses in college.

Making new friends in college is not as difficult as it seems. Everyone is just starting out. Everyone is looking to meet new people. In fact, entering freshmen have in one sense been offered a new lease on life. No one knows your reputation—good or bad— from high school. In fact, the freshman year is an opportune time to change your image, especially if negative opinions have tarnished it.

For example, the high-school student who sloughed off studies or put down others can begin a college career with renewed enthusiasm, an energetic vigor for the intellectual life, and a wholesome openness to and appreciation for other people. He or she can abandon the trivial high-school mind games and be the beautiful, unique, and good person he or she really is.

Here are some pointers on making friends:

- First, a word of caution: Be careful not to latch on to your first campus acquaintance. Sometimes people lower their standards because they so desire any kind of relationship or they fear they won't find someone else. You have heard this advice before: Be patient.

  Never do anything that makes you uncomfortable or that is wrong just to keep a friend. Ben Franklin advised, "Be slow in choosing a friend, slower in changing."

- Make yourself available. Expand beyond your high-school circle of friends. You are bound to find new friends if you try things like sitting in the rows of classes with other students and not by yourself, joining others at a cafeteria table, or participating in the social events sponsored by the orientation committee.

- Be yourself. Your honesty and sincerity will attract likewise authentic friends.

- Be a good listener. Ask questions that focus on the other person: Where did you go to high school? What is your major? Why did you choose this college? Make eye contact with the person as he or she is speaking. Don't interrupt. Occasionally rephrase what the other person said. This shows you are interested and that you are indeed listening.

- Smile. A smile conveys warmth and good cheer. People like to be around those who are optimistic and happy.

- Develop your friendship with Jesus. Spend some time each day in prayer listening to Jesus. Read the scriptures. Share your concerns with him. If you imitate Jesus by becoming a thoughtful, caring, sensitive individual, others will note those qualities in you.

- Friendship equals commitment. Realize that developing and maintaining a friendship requires time, energy, and love.
Friendship involves both giving and receiving. Being there for a friend helps sustain and intensify your relationship. Therefore, be sure to factor time into your schedule to cultivate your friendships.

Dealing with Differences

"When you starts measuring somebody, measure him right. . . . Make sure you done taken into account what hills and valleys he come through before he got wherever he is."

—Mama speaking to her son in
Act 3 of the play, *A Raisin in the Sun*, by Lorraine Hansberry

One phenomenon you will notice immediately when arriving on a college campus is the great diversity among students. You will have classmates who are not only from a different place than you, but they will come from different religions and socio-economic backgrounds than you. They will be a rainbow of races who trace their national identity to different countries and hold a host of political views. Some of your classmates will be homosexual. Others will have physical challenges. In addition, if you went to an all-boys or all-girls school, you will likely now have classmates of the opposite gender.

Most colleges have students from every part of the country

and from many other countries around the world. These students have a myriad of interests and a smorgasbord of appealing talents. You will quickly notice more distinct clothing, hair styles, and places for body piercings than you ever could have imagined. Some of your fellow students will flaunt their distinctiveness to underscore their desire to be individuals.

How should you react to all this? First, remain calm! Meeting, interacting with, and learning from different people is a major goal of undergraduate education. We live in a pluralistic society where people from various backgrounds and widely varying views have agreed to live together in peace and harmony. This ideal social compact is, of course, sometimes tough to put into practice. Colleges are not immune to the problems of the larger society. Racial tensions exist on college campuses. Homosexuals are targeted for violence and abuse. Vandalism occurs.

As you know, this illegal and immoral behavior is contrary to Jesus' law of love of neighbor. A life-giving truth Jesus revealed is that *all* people—no matter race, nationality, creed, or sexual orientation—are members of one human family. Thus, we are children of a compassionately loving God and brothers and sisters in Jesus Christ. Reacting to others not as aliens or enemies, but as real brothers and sisters, helps us accept and even appreciate God's plan of human diversity.

One positive way to embrace the differences in people you experience is to look at these encounters as learning opportunities. Meeting and knowing different kinds of people can open you up to new ways of perceiving reality. More important, these people can become your friends.

Prejudice—judging someone on insufficient evidence—is the one barrier that can make it impossible to be open to those who are different. Prejudice is learned behavior. It thrives on stereotyping, that is, judging a person or a whole group of people by exaggerating one trait or quality. It manifests itself in un-Christian behavior like verbal abuse (e.g., telling racial jokes), avoidance, discrimination, physical violence, and even killing. Prejudice, however, can be overcome: it can be unlearned through exposure with an open mind to different kinds of people and to then accepting them as individuals.

Finally, do you need to accept everything about a person who is different? No. Obviously, some qualities a person has no control over—sex, race, nationality, the region from which he or she comes. To reject a person because of these externals is narrow-minded, wrong, and even sinful. But people do have control over their *behavior*. For example, you can accept, respect, and love a person who has a homosexual orientation. Most people do not choose this orientation. But you don't have to buy into the secular philosophy that homosexual *behavior* is moral and a licit option for human relationships. Being open-minded is not equivalent to an "anything goes" philosophy. Christians are called to love all people. However, Christians do not have to accept behaviors or political views or practices that are destructive, harmful, and sinful.

Joining Up

The difficulty in life is the choice.

—George Mooren

Shortly after you arrive on campus—perhaps as part of your orientation—the myriad activities available to you as an undergraduate will vie for your attention. Should you join a club or participate in an activity? If so, how many? These two questions will demand an answer in your first month at college.

Think of all the extracurricular offerings as part of a buffet table. The trouble with eating from a buffet table is the tendency to overindulge. A bloat of extracurricular activities is not something you need your first semester of college. Always keep in mind that your top priority is academics. Everything else is secondary.

Consider signing up for just *one* activity your first semester. In choosing an activity, ask yourself: How will this activity help me grow as a person? How will this activity help me become more well-rounded? What benefit does it have for my future, especially my career or vocation?

When choosing an activity, seriously think about one that is service-oriented. Serving others helps you take your mind off yourself and your own problems. For example, what really helped me my first semester away from home was getting up every Sunday morning to teach catechism classes at an inner-city parish. The discipline of serving youngsters helped me overcome homesickness. I was in control of something; at the same time, it made me feel good about myself in my new surroundings. I was doing good for others. A wise person summarized it well: "Service is the price we pay for the space we occupy."

If you decide to engage in an activity your first semester, be faithful to the time commitment it requires. People will depend on you. This is another reason not to overindulge in extracurricular activities until you know what you can handle. After your first-semester grades come in, reassess your extracurricular involvement. Adjust your commitments accordingly.

Having started this chapter with the questions of Robert Fulghum, take some time to analyze the rules he and probably you learned in kindergarten. These rules are valuable even for college freshmen:[3]

▼ ▼ ▼ ▼ ▼

1. Play fair.

2. Don't hit people.

3. Put things back where you found them.

4. Clean up your own mess.

5. Don't take things that aren't yours.

6. Say you're sorry when you hurt somebody.

7. Wash your hands before you eat.

8. Take a nap every day.

9. Flush.

▲ ▲ ▲ ▲ ▲

Three
HITTING THE BOOKS

A diligent freshman went to her first English Literature class and sat in the front row. The professor immediately told the class that they would be reading five books during the term, and that he would be giving them a list of authors from which to choose. Then, he went to the lectern, opened his class book, and rattled off some names: "Abbot, Bruce, Carey, Carson, Dooley. . . ."

The conscientious freshman feverishly began to scribble down the names in her notebook. Moments later, she felt a tap on her shoulder from the guy sitting behind her. "Don't jot notes. He's only taking attendance."[1]

The freshman may have been a bit overzealous, but she certainly realized that one key to academic success is the taking of good class notes. This chapter will treat some topics of vital interest for academic success, including:

- ▸ Choosing a major
- ▸ Time management
- ▸ Going to class
- ▸ Study tips
- ▸ Test-taking
- ▸ Writing papers

Choosing a Major

One should be able to distinguish between
good, bad, and downright awful.
—Isaiah Berlin

The most popular major for college freshmen is "undecided." Should this be a source of concern at this stage of your life? No. The president of a Jesuit university told me that the average undergraduate changes majors three times during college. Even if you have already "decided" on one major, that does not guarantee that you will graduate with the same one.

As you consider making a decision about a college major, ask yourself this fundamental question about the reason for a college education: Is it to prepare you for a living or to prepare you for life?

The issue is not really what you are going to *do* with your life. The central question is what are you going to *be*. What kind of person do you wish to become?

The rush to choose a major is often a symptom of society's desire to have you fit into the system. This system lionizes material wealth, unthinking consumerism, and blind acceptance of the superficial status quo.

An educated Christian will at least pause and ask: "Why am I really majoring in this subject? Is it merely a stepping stone to an easy life? Or is it a means to a good life—a life of serving other people?"

Take some time to wrestle with these foundational questions because they are more important for your ultimate happiness than your choice of a major. Meanwhile, concentrate on taking courses in the core subjects, for example, English, foreign languages, and math or science. Leave room for an additional elective or two to help you experience what might later become a major course of study.

If possible, sign up for an outstanding professor, an excellent teacher who excites students about the subject matter. (Consult with a couple of serious-minded juniors or seniors. They'll be glad to level with you.) The course title is not important for profs like this. Their joyful presentation of their field may very well be the catalyst that will turn you on to a new course of study never considered before.

Here are two other helps for choosing a major:

1. Seek God's plan for your life.

The key to both happiness and holiness is doing God's will. How often do you pray "Thy will be done" in the Lord's Prayer, yet make your own plans and then petition God to support them? This is doing things backward and can really lead to unhappiness and confusion. Being in "sync" with God's plan is a much surer path to peace and happiness.

Your most basic decision starting out in college is not the choice of a major but the choice to follow God's plan for your life. To sincerely pray "Thy will be done" means paying attention to the details and larger story of your life and how God is working in it. Spend time in prayer discerning God's will for you. This means asking yourself:

▸ What are your deepest inclinations? What subjects and topics really engage you? Ordinarily, God works through these attractions and likely implanted them in you in the first place.

- When two possible choices confront you, which—in your imagination—brings you the most peace? Which seems the more natural fit for your personality and talents? If you are truly doing God's will, you will experience a profound sense that what you decided is right.

2. Reflect on your interests.

Part of what college is all about is to continue to discover your talents and to think about different ways you can use them to serve others and make a relatively happy life for yourself.

Many students choose majors based on their gut-level reaction to certain subjects they've taken in school in the past. Their instincts are often a good guide, especially if they correspond to a real love for the subject matter in a particular field. Pay attention to your instincts as you take various courses. Can they be telling you something about yourself? For example:

Are you an idea person? Does thinking, reading, talking, and writing about ideas turn you on? Do you like solving problems? Are you good at communicating your thoughts? Do you like debating themes in movies, editorials, books you read? If so, then philosophy, English, or the sciences might be a good major for you.

Are you a people person? Do you like learning why people and societies act the way they do? Are you outgoing? Do you love to talk to and associate with people? Do you empathize with others, putting yourself in their place and looking at issues from their point of view? Do you want to deal with lots of people on a daily basis? If so, maybe you should think about teaching, nursing, psychology, sociology, or one of the performing arts.

Do you like to tinker with things? Are you a computer whiz? Do you like taking things apart and putting them back together? Do you like to express your intelligence through things you've made or discovered? Are you curious about how the natural world operates? If so, the physical and natural sciences or experimental psychology or various arts may be for you.

Choosing a major by assessing your talents and paying attention to your own natural likes and dislikes is as good a method as any to making this key decision. Remember that your freshman year is a good time to monitor what attracts you. There will be plenty of time in later years to think about how you can translate your major into a job. Now is the time to throw yourself into college life and enjoy the many opportunities.

Also know that choosing a college major is not your ultimate decision in life. Many professionals and happy and well-adjusted people are working in fields totally unrelated to their college majors. For example, I have had students who majored in English and are now surgeons, or majored in music and are now successful entrepreneurs, or majored in business and are teaching religion full-time.

But for many others, there is some definite relationship between their college major and their careers. There are likely more doctors who majored in biology than English.

Think of your college degree as a credential that can help put you on a career path. It cannot *guarantee* that you will be a psychologist or a lawyer or an accountant. For many careers, you will need advanced education in graduate or professional school or as an apprentice on the job.

Sometimes your performance in certain courses can limit your choices for a college major. Many freshmen begin the year majoring in biology or chemistry with the intention of becoming doctors. But a below-average grade or extreme difficulty in the required course convinced them the major and career wasn't for them. Use your own capacity to handle certain subjects academically, emotionally, and physically to help you choose a major course of study.

Planning: Time Management

There are thinkers and doers.
Then, there are those who think a lot about doing.
—Anonymous

There are at least four types of freshmen who roam the campus. *Drifters* have no sense of direction. They lack self-discipline and are easily distracted by others. *Dreamers* are subject to wishful and usually unrealistic thinking. They are controlled by a "shoulda, coulda, woulda" mentality. *Demons* are hell-bent on having fun. Nothing much else matters to these restless souls. *Doers* are different from the rest. They are self-directed and organized. Doers succeed. They pay a price for success, but to them the gain is worth the pain. They have a plan, and they sacrifice to stick to it.

A major part of a doer's success is effective *time management*. Conscientiously managing time is a necessity for a college student. It helps you:

- set priorities for the day, week, month, and semester ahead
- avoid conflicts
- evaluate your progress for test preparation, doing major projects, and writing papers
- take advantage of opportunities (e.g., knowing when to use limited resources like books on the library reserve shelf)
- dodge those anxious "I'm-always-behind-and-don't know-where-I'm-going" feelings
- study smarter, not harder
- be in control

For doers, college is like a job with a 45-hour work week. Forty-five hours is a realistic goal given the 168 total hours in a week. Here's how a basic time management plan might break down:

classes	15	
studying	30	
church	1	
sleep	56	(8 hours per night)
socializing/eating	21	(3 hours per day)
free time	45	(equivalent of another work week)
Total	168	

A difference between college and high school is that in college you are only in class about three or four hours a day. Compare this to the typical eight-hour high-school day. Also, you have a seven-day period, not five, to stretch out your 30 hours of studying.

One survey discovered that less than 25 percent of full-time college students study more than 16 hours per week. Imagine how well you will do if you stick to a realistic work schedule. Note a big payoff to this suggested time control: having fun without sacrificing good grades.

Organize your time according to the following principles and you are bound to succeed:

1. Work for A's in all courses during your first semester.

Most of your classmates won't do this, so you will stand out. By committing yourself to this goal first semester, you'll know what it takes to get high grades. You may decide later that it is not worth putting in the kind of time necessary to get a 3.8 grade point average, for example. Nevertheless, you'll never know what is needed for this level of accomplishment unless you commit yourself to this goal early in your career. Even if you don't attain your goal, your disciplined work habits will get you off to an excellent start.

2. Create a homework schedule and always stick to it.

Remember to treat college as if it were a job. If you fail to do the work adequately you will eventually lose the job. Cut out study time and you'll eventually pay for it as severely. You may remember this experience as a high-school student: you regretted not spending an extra few minutes studying for an exam when you eventually missed a higher grade by only one or two percentage points. Analyze this situation and make the necessary corrections in college.

3. Work ahead of schedule.

Likely in a given week, especially at the start of the semester, you won't have 30 hours of homework. Great! Use the chance to work ahead. Most professors assign major projects or papers at the beginning of a semester. Use the light schedule in the early weeks to do preliminary research and writing. Or, read ahead in the assigned texts. Doing so will help you profit much more from a prof's lecture. Being ahead of the game also allows you to handle emergencies like sickness or unexpected surprises like a visit from a high-school friend.

CALENDARS AND CHARTS

Time management is a matter of organization. Obtain and use the following to help you get organized and remain organized through each term:

- Large wall calendar. After you have reviewed all of your syllabi, list on this calendar the deadlines for tests, lab reports, term papers, and major homework assignments. Use a different color ink for each subject. Note common due dates and begin immediately to map out strategies for handling the glut of work. *Suggestion:* Create your own *earlier* deadlines for big projects like term papers.

- Flow chart/project board. This is especially helpful for the systematic planning of term papers. List your own deadlines for completing topic selection, initial library research, first outline, further library research, revised outline, rough draft, proofing by self and another, and final draft. Allow a week before the scheduled due date to have everything completed to create cushion time in case of emergencies.

- Monthly desk calendar. Transcribe the data from the wall calendar onto your desk calendar. Add homework assignments and other obligations that you'll have during the month.

- Pocket daily schedule with hour-by-hour listings. Fill each hour for the coming week on Sunday night and revise as needed during the week. Follow this plan:

— Make a "to-do" list, ranking high- to low-priority obligations. Cross off items as you accomplish them. This will give you a psychological boost, a feeling of progress.

— Include fixed times like classes, meals, errands, meetings, exercise, and time for socializing and prayer. But be sure to factor in four to five hours of good study time per day, Monday through Thursday. This will help you go a long way toward meeting the suggested 30 hours per week of study time. Plan your weekend to suit your social life, but also allow for about eight hours of weekend study.

— Schedule your study times for when you have the most energy. Be specific. For example, in your 7 to 8:30 pm slot, instead of writing "study psychology," write "read psych text, chapter 5."

— Stick to the study time you write in the pocket schedule.

— Look at your *daily* schedule every day, first thing in the morning. This will help you plan your day efficiently. For example, take what you need for the trip to the library between your first two classes along with your class supplies. This will save you wasted steps and time going back to retrieve them from your dorm room or car.

In the Classroom

It's easier to keep up than to catch up.
—an "A" student

College classes are organized and scheduled much differently than high-school classes. Some introductory lecture classes are in large halls with more than one hundred students; other small seminar groups have as few as three or four students. Compared to high school, college classes meet less frequently, at most only three times a week. Some evening courses assemble only once a week. College courses typically require long-term projects, with little daily homework. Don't be surprised if a given course has only two exams, a midterm and final with each being worth half of your grade.

The self-discipline needed for success in college begins with going to class. Many professors don't take attendance. There is no dean of students to hassle you about not coming to class. You have to be in charge of your education from being present in class through studying, writing papers, working on individual or group projects, and passing exams. Remember this important lesson: Academic success begins by being present. Here are some keys to get you off to a good start:

Attend class. Regular class attendance is vital for good grades. You can't expect to rely on the note-taking of a friend to get you through. Rather, be present at the beginning of each session for important review. Stay to the end of the session when quizzes and assignments are often given. By now you should have discovered that grading has a subjective element to it. Regular class attendance *does* influence many professors to perceive you in a positive light. Profs often give the benefit of doubt to those who show an interest in their courses.

Allow your profs the chance to get to know you by face and name. Sitting front and center has three major benefits:

1. It will enable you to make eye contact with the prof.

2. It will help you avoid distractions, like daydreaming and looking out of the window.

3. It will allow you more direct access when you want to participate.

By the way, don't hesitate to participate by asking questions. The only dumb question is the unasked one. Questions show you are interested, and they help clarify information for you and your classmates.

Attendance on the first day of the term is especially important. Make sure you understand the items on the syllabus. If your prof fails to provide a syllabus, ask for one or at least make sure of the elements that go into your grade. How many tests are there? Does the course require a paper? Will the final be comprehensive? Do homework assignments factor into the grade? Will the prof give extra credit? These are all important questions that should be answered on the first day.

Come to class prepared. Make sure you read the assigned texts ahead of time and that you review your notes from the previous class. These two simple techniques will help you follow along with the lecture much easier. Recall one of the rules for academic success: Work ahead of schedule (but not too far so that you will forget).

Take good notes. Use a separate 8 1/2" x 11" size notebook for each course. Write your name, address, and phone number in it in case of loss. Date your notes for each day you are in class. Take notes in outline form to help you see the flow of the presentations as developed by the lecturer. Allow yourself enough space for your own questions, notes, and thoughts.

Use a good-flowing pen to help you write quickly. Always keep a backup pen on hand.

Pay close attention to the various hints profs give to underscore what is important and notable. Copy *everything* they write on the board into your notebook. Be on the lookout for buzz phrases like, "This is important," or "I can't stress enough. . . ." Profs also clue test items with phrases like, "Is this clear?" or, "Is there anyone who doesn't understand this?"

For your daily note-taking, put the lecture into your own words by summarizing the main ideas and giving examples. Really try to understand what the prof is saying. Always note definitions and jot down lists or enumerated points. Underline your notes or use asterisks for points of emphasis.

Review class lectures as soon as possible. Some say we are not able to retain 50 percent of processed information within the first hour. The most productive review time is right after class. Review, rewrite, and

summarize class notes daily. Go back over the lecture with a highlighter to emphasize key points. Then compress these highlights to a few summary statements that will help you remember the major ideas.

Seek help if you are confused. If you don't understand something, meet with the prof outside of class. The course syllabus usually gives his or her office hours and the telephone numbers to schedule an appointment. Admitting that you need help is certainly better than carrying doubts into the day of the test.

Study Tips

Today's preparation determines
tomorrow's achievement.

—from a Valedictorian's address

Success in college is directly proportional to productive study sessions. A comfortable study area and consistent study time are necessary preconditions for two necessary study skills: fruitful text reading and memorizing information to prepare for tests.

The Study Area

How lucky for you if your dorm room is quiet enough so that you can study in it. If not, then stake a claim to a table in a dorm study room, a carrel in the library, or a desk in an empty classroom, providing it is a designated and safe area for study. Wherever you end up studying regularly, you will want to make it accessible, convenient, and pleasant. Basics include a comfortable chair, decent lighting, good ventilation, and a cool temperature (if it is too hot, you will fall asleep). Many people like to study with music in the background because it serves as "white noise" that camouflages other distracting sounds. Familiar instrumental music with steady rhythms is less distracting than music with lyrics, a variety of rhythms, and high decibels.

Distractions are the curse of serious students. Reduce them by unplugging the phone and avoiding television. If you find your study sessions unproductive, try changing the environment. It may be as simple as rearranging the top of your desk or finding an alternative study area. It is a good idea to have a backup place for those times when a study session is not going well because of one distraction or another. A change of scenery may help you refocus and settle down.

What Time Is Best for Study?

Everyone has a peak time for doing the most productive studying, a block of time in the morning or in the evening. Determine when you study best and make this time sacrosanct. Reserve up to four consecutive hours. Stick to this study time, even when you don't feel like studying. It will give you an edge over those who decide to study just when they "feel" like it.

Work on your most difficult, least favorite, or highest-priority assignment first. Allot enough time to finish or make significant progress on this difficult task before moving on to another. Don't rush through one assignment just to get to another.

You will find your study sessions more productive if you study dissimilar subject areas back-to-back. For example, work some math problems after reading a history chapter. By the way, it's usually less fatiguing to do text reading *before* doing interactive work like math problems.

When your studying is going well, reward yourself with frequent breaks, say a ten-minute break for each 45 minutes of study. (But avoid watching television during a break or you might get hooked on a program that will torpedo your good resolve.) After a tough week of study (e.g., for a midterm or final exam), add a special reward like purchasing a CD, taking in a movie, or making two or three phone calls to old friends. Be sure to break up all study times with exercise. Exercise relieves tension and helps you to think more clearly.

Don't limit your study time simply to the scheduled peak energy period. Capture a spare half-hour here or there between classes for text reading. One estimate claims that college students are assigned an average of ten pages of reading per day in each class. With five courses, you may be required to read over 50 pages per day in a wide range of subject areas and difficulty. This task can be overwhelming. Stealing time between classes can help to lessen the load.

Finally, be sure to leave enough study time for tests. Your best preparation for exams is to review faithfully and intelligently your class notes each day. Allow at least two nights to study for a regular exam, approximately six hours on average. Add more time related to the weight of the exam and the difficulty you have in mastering a particular subject area.

How to Read a Text

Reading a textbook is a different kind of reading than when you read a novel you enjoy. You will be asked to prove comprehension of text material in some form, usually an exam. Three simple words characterize a good approach to text reading: *overview*, *view*, and *review*.

A good start to a text reading assignment is to initially *overview* the chapter or assignment. Skim the headings and subheadings. Note highlighted material, including charts or illustrations. Five minutes spent acclimating yourself to the material may be very beneficial. Read any summary statements or questions at the end of a section.

Read or *view* at a good clip so that you don't get bogged down in minute details. Use a bright yellow highlighter for marking terms, definitions, and key points. (Avoid underlining with a ruler since it is too mechanical and time-consuming.) Highlight no more than a third of the material or you'll defeat the purpose of highlighting which is to extract only essential information. Draw arrows or stars in the margins to call attention to more important examples or essential points. Place question marks next to paragraphs that confuse you. Plan to ask about this material in class.

Most important, read for understanding. Jot points into your notebook putting the main ideas into your own words. Look at headings and subheadings and imagine them as test questions. Write several who, what, why, and how questions. Read the text to get answers to your own questions.

Review the material you highlighted. Condense it to the main points and write these points in your notebook. Concentrate on learning and remembering these points. Also, answer any study questions provided in the chapter. These help you review and check whether you grasp the main concepts. Besides, profs like to re-form study questions and use them on texts.

Memorizing Material for Tests

Before you begin to memorize material for a test, make sure it's correct. Check and match your class and text notes with study guide information and text summaries. Next, organize your time for fruitful study sessions. Periodic sessions of 15 to 20 minutes in duration are more productive than two-hour sessions of straight memorizing. A good time to memorize information is just prior to going to sleep. Follow up with a review immediately after waking up.

Effective memorization involves all of your senses. Look at your notes (sight), rewrite your notes by condensing (touch), and say your notes aloud (hearing). I used this method effectively when I was a college student. First, I would condense all my notes to a page or two. Then I'd read them repeatedly, making sure I really understood the concepts. (Understanding makes memorizing easier and is the purpose of learning.) Finally, I'd take a walk, saying the notes aloud until I had them memorized. I'd test my retention by speaking the notes aloud until I was confident I knew them.

Other helpful hints for memorization:

- *Create anagrams.* An anagram is a word made by the first letters of the words of a phrase. Your anagrams don't have to be *real* words. They only need to be words that *you* can easily remember. For example, I still remember an anagram that I created to describe Wordsworth's nineteenth-century concept of Romantic spirit: **SOOPERIT** ("spontaneous overflow of powerful emotion recollected in tranquillity")!

- *Use different colored highlight markers for review notes.* Creative page layout is an effective way to better envision your notes.

- *Cluster.* Group apparent isolated facts, numbers, and letters into clusters. It is tough to remember 265837466; it is easier to remember 265 837 466.

- Avoid *"cramming."* Last-minute study heightens anxiety and is not conducive to retaining information.

Study Groups and Seeking Help

Some students derive great benefit by participating in study groups with other students. However, study groups should never substitute for doing your own homework, text-reading, or problem-solving. An ideal size for a study group is four to six members. Hopefully the other members of the group will be as talented, serious-minded, and hard-working as you, if not more so. This means that members come to a study group session well-prepared. For example, they compose and answer possible test questions, drill essential material, and create anagrams to help remember key concepts.

Be sure to look into a study group sponsored by the course's prof or grad assistants. Usually these groups can walk you through some practice exams and help you focus on skills needed to pass an upcoming text.

Also, don't be ashamed if you are struggling in a course. Get help *before* you fail! If early intervention does not help you improve your grade you should have time to drop the course. (However, note that many colleges allow the dropping and adding of courses only in the first week or two of a semester.)

Make an appointment with your professor; most are eager to help struggling students. Follow their recommendation: join a study group, seek a tutor, go to the campus academic services center. The campus life office or student affairs center will suggest many resources at your college to help you get through a tough course.

Test-Taking Tips

When you get to the end of your rope,
tie a knot and hang on.

—Franklin D. Roosevelt

Here's a quick fact: the average college student takes about 130 exams from freshman year to graduation. You can't get through college without passing more than a few tests! A good test assesses student learning in a challenging yet fair way. Tests are time-honored methods to get feedback on the effectiveness of the teaching-learning process. This section lists some ways to survive college tests.

Preparation

Your best way to prepare for tests is to review your class and text notes on a *weekly* basis, trying to discover what you know and don't know. As part of this review, condense your notes, create anagrams, and verbalize the material. An excellent preparation technique is to anticipate test questions and to practice answering them. Study groups or study partners can be especially helpful in creating these practice questions.

Prepare especially well for the first test in a course. A good grade on the first test will get you off to a good start and help you "bank" points for later exams.

Get a good night's sleep before a test. Review your study notes on the morning of the test. For a longer testing period, bring a high-protein snack and drink. Also, bring a watch to help keep up a good pace during the exam.

When You Are Given the Test

Read over the entire test when you receive it. Carefully note the directions (e.g., you may need to answer only *some* of the essays). Allot the proper time for relative value of each section of the test.

Circle or check the numbers of the harder questions. Leave them for later. Completing some of the easier questions will help answer the more difficult ones.

For *objective* or *multiple choice* tests, read the directions carefully. Note that sometimes the prof wants the *best* answer from among several "good" answers. Look for choices with qualifiers like "always" and "never." They are usually not correct. Also, if your test has been created by the professor (versus computer-generated), look for the right answer among the middle choices (e.g., B or C) rather than the first or last choices (e.g., A or D).

For the more difficult test items, cross out any obviously wrong choices. Narrow down the choices as much as possible. If two choices are exactly opposite, one of them is probably the correct one. If you have trouble finally choosing, read the question and each choice as an independent statement. Your first guess is usually correct.

Finally, about every five questions, verify that you are marking the right line on the answer sheet.

The good news about *true-false* tests is that you have a 50 percent chance of guessing correctly. Note that many longer true-false statements and ones with qualifiers like "sometimes," "generally," and "usually" tend to be true. On the other hand, those with absolutes like "always" and "never" are typically false.

Fill-in tests are more difficult than multiple choice and true-false tests because they challenge your recall. Unlike essay questions, fill-in answers require preciseness, not writing around the issue with wordy sentences. For fill-in tests, write something in the blank even if you are not sure. The prof may give you some credit for creative thinking. If the answer is literally on the tip of your tongue, go through the alphabet letter-by-letter. It may help to trigger your memory.

Essay tests require you to know exactly what is being asked before you begin writing. Don't hesitate to ask your prof to clarify a confusing term or unclear question before you begin to write. Then, decide how much time you will spend on each essay, assigning more time to the essays that count the most.

Spend a few minutes outlining your essay answer on scratch paper. Organization and neatness do count and impress. Some professors will lower your grade if your logic is confusing or they develop eyestrain trying to decipher sloppy handwriting.

Then follow this format for essay answers: (1) *Tell 'em what you're gonna tell 'em* (the introduction), (2) *Tell 'em* (the body), and (3) *Tell 'em what you told 'em* (the conclusion).

In the introduction, define your terms. In the body, make your best point first, use examples, and, if possible, quote your professor. (In general, on tests you should agree with the points of view expressed by your prof. Use class discussions for controversial opinions that contradict what your prof is advocating.) In the conclusion, quickly summarize your points.

If you draw a total blank, try to write *something*. Compassionate professors or their graduate assistants will often give you partial credit.

Coping with Test Anxiety

Test-taking is stressful. There is no way to completely avoid the anxiety that accompanies this activity. However, some anxiety-reducing measures can help.

First, arrive to class early. Choose a good seat away from drafty windows and long-winded friends. In fact, it's a good idea to avoid your other classmates altogether. Their pre-test chit-chat and last-minute cramming can prove to be a distraction.

When you receive the test, divide your time according to the relative value of each section of the text. Ignore the test-taking pace of others. Some people flip pages quickly because they are totally lost and anxious to leave the testing room.

If you freeze up, answer the easy questions first for a confidence boost. Remind yourself that you are demonstrating what you *know*, not what you don't know.

Don't leave the testing room early. Review the test items if you finish ahead of time. For example, retake the objective items, covering your original answers. You may catch one or more mistakes you originally made.

Finally, keep the test in perspective. You've studied your best and given your complete effort. Put the test in perspective according to your total grade in the course. Also, how well or poorly you did ultimately has little cosmic significance. For example, picture yourself 70 years from now on your deathbed. I seriously doubt that you will care how well you did on a given test. When the testing period is over and you leave the room, try not to give it another thought.

8 **Smart** Things College Freshmen Do

Say "no" to many commitments

Plan ahead by stating realistic goals, outlining tasks needed to execute them, and finding a way to check progress

8 **Dumb** Things College Freshmen Do

Procrastinate

Refuse to set goals or make calendars

Have a regular study time and stick to it	Pull all-nighters
Go to class	Cut classes
Do extra work	Watch a lot of television
Work ahead	Put off until later what can be done today
Socialize as a reward for good study	Party during the week
Maintain a support system (linked with family)	Go it alone

Writing Papers

To err is human, to have a word processor that allows
you to correct mistakes without an eraser is divine.
—adapted from Shakespeare

You will write many papers in college: themes, critical essays, reflections, reports, reaction papers, take-home exams, and of course, the infamous term papers. Each academic department has its own style for written papers, and individual professors have their own quirks on how they want you to write papers for their classes. Attend to these departmental and professorial guidelines as a first step in writing an acceptable paper.

An equally important first step is to *start your papers early*. "Paper procrastination" is a common disease among college students. The problem is multiplied to dangerous degrees when dealing with term papers. The writing of a term paper requires that you identify a worthwhile topic, read a great deal of information, organize and synthesize discrete pieces of information, and report your quotes and sources in an intelligent, accurate, and disciplined manner. The purpose of a term paper is to teach you *how* to learn: to retrieve information, to develop critical thinking skills, and to integrate knowledge. In short, it is hard work, and that's a common reason why some students procrastinate.

The plan of attack for writing a term paper always includes being organized from start to finish. Check the library for information on potential topics. Also, scan the Internet for other outstanding available resources. You can call up references through a menu service called Gopher that allows you access to up-to-date research from college campuses across the nation.

Regardless of how you gather information, it is imperative to transfer a summary of the information to 4" x 6" note cards and the references of the material cited to 3" x 5" index cards. The material on these cards becomes the main source of information for your paper. You can easily arrange and rearrange the cards as you create and revise your outline.

Develop an outline with headings and subheadings for major divisions. Headings break up long pages of type and reveal to the reader your logic and organization. Many college papers are sloppy and rambling. Headings and subheadings help to end this.

Compose your papers on a computer. Not only can you save them for future reference, a word processing program enables you to revise your work easily, format footnotes automatically, and check spelling and grammar.

A prime advantage to starting your term papers early is that you can put your first draft aside for a few days before rewriting it. (For too many students, their first draft is their *final* draft. Profs easily recognize this type of effort.) Giving your paper a fresh look after a few days can help you make effective refinements. An early start will also allow you to get a classmate to read and critique a first draft. A second or third pair of eyes on a paper is a valuable help and can dramatically help you to improve the final draft.

Also, by starting early you will have time to seek out the professor or grad assistant for help. Finally, as columnist William Safire, reminds you, avoid bad grammar. His "Fumblerules of Grammar" should help you to this end:

Don't use no double negatives.

Proofread carefully to see if you any words out.

Take the bull by the hand and avoid mixed metaphors.

If I've told you once, I've told you a thousand times, resist hyperbole.

Avoid commas, that are not necessary.

Avoid clichés like the plague.

Never use a long word when a diminutive will do.

Avoid colloquial stuff.

Four

CHALLENGES AND DILEMMAS OF COLLEGE LIFE

Jack Canfield, co-author of the very popular Chicken Soup for the Soul *series, tells of watching a Little League baseball game near his home. He asked one of the little boys what the score was.*

Smiling, the boy replied, "We're losing 14-0."

"Aren't you discouraged?" asked Canfield.

"Discouraged?" the boy replied. "Why should we be discouraged? We haven't been up to bat yet."[1]

This marvelous story teaches the value of a positive attitude to help overcome seemingly insurmountable odds. A positive attitude not only helps a little kid stay in the game, it can help a college freshman deal with the tough problems and decisions that inevitably are part of the college scene. This chapter focuses on some challenging issues, including:

- Dealing with troublesome profs

- Deciding whether or not to pledge sororities or fraternities

- Handling dating, love, and sexual feelings in appropriate ways
- Understanding the ramifications of alcohol and drugs
- Responding to the widespread practice of cheating on college campuses.

College Professors: Handle with Care

A teacher affects eternity;
he can never tell where his influence stops.

—Henry Brooks Adams

A recent survey discovered that the four top fears of most people are (1) making a speech, (2) getting fat, (3) being around high or exposed places, and (4) going to the dentist. To this list college students often add the fear of being stuck with a demanding, insensitive, or unreasonable professor.

With luck, you won't get any professor with those characteristics during your college years. Usually, you will enroll in courses with competent, fair, and knowledgeable profs. Sometimes, you will be fortunate enough to land some truly great professors. Experts in their fields, they expect excellence from you and evoke it through their example rather than through intimidation. They are patient and empathetic. And they love the art of teaching, their subject matter, and students of all ability levels. When you run into professors like this, sign up for more than one course that they offer. They make going to college exciting and mind-stretching.

You can work toward a good relationship with most college professors simply by observing common courtesies, including the following:

✔ Address your professors by their correct titles. Some are very sensitive if you do not call them "Doctor." You will find other profs who are more informal and won't mind you calling them by their first name. But let them invite you to use this more casual approach.

- ✔ Be on time for class. Tardiness does not go unnoticed. It annoys and distracts lecturers. If you are going to be late, enter the room unobtrusively.

- ✔ Read the syllabus and know course policies. This will save misunderstandings down the line.

- ✔ Participate in class discussions. When appropriate, ask intelligent questions. Be attentive in class and show it by making eye contact. There is nothing more reassuring to a teacher than to have students who "connect" by paying attention and who give some type of feedback through good eye contact, occasionally nodding the head, or by asking a stimulating question.

- ✔ When appropriate, compliment the professor for an outstanding lecture. Cynics might call this "schmoozing" or, more crudely, "brown-nosing." More charitably, Christian decency requires that we acknowledge the superior contributions of others—peers or mentors.

- ✔ Refuse to rationalize for late or inadequate work. These rationalizations might have worked in high school, but college professors can see through transparent sophomoric excuses. There is no substitute for hard work, promptly delivered. Professors notice and reward such effort.

- ✔ A former student wrote with this excellent advice: "Make sure you talk to your teacher if you are having problems or even if you are not. Let them know you are interested in their classes. This will often help you receive a better grade on the final report card."

- ✔ Get to know the profs in your major field of study. Remember that down the line in your academic career someone will have to write a letter of recommendation for you. You must know and befriend at least some of your professors. One way of doing this is to express an interest in a prof's research and ask to participate in some way. Many professors love to mentor students interested in their field of expertise.

Following the above tips should help you maintain a good relationship with most of your professors whether they are up-to-date experts or fossils in their field, great teachers or poor communicators, available or distant, parsimonious or generous graders, excited about teaching or bored with it.

However, as psychologist and veteran college teacher Christopher F. Monte warns, there are several types of professors who need special care: the arrogant, the narcissistic, the indifferent, and the obsessive professors.[2] Incidentally, a great advantage of going to an optional summer orientation is to find out from older students which profs to avoid. If you do wind up with one of the types of professors described by Monte, he offers some advice on how to recognize and cope with each of these professor types.

Arrogant profs, he writes, have a distorted sense of their own achievement. They are insecure and must display their "superior" intelligence to be accepted. They are basically angry and don't like others to best them.

These professors have a knack for angering their students. Work to keep your anger in check. Recognize that such professors have a poor self-image and are hurting inside because of their insecurity. They are not superior to you. A Christian response would be to be kind to these professors and respect what they can teach you. They probably have achieved some academic goal and can have something worthwhile to offer you. Avoid taking them for a future course.

Narcissistic profs are sad with very fragile and easily-wounded self-images. They are oversensitive to others' reactions to them. They are self-absorbed, self-focused, and hungry for love. They abhor competition from their students.

Ignoring or snubbing narcissistic professors is dangerous. Listen carefully to them. Make eye contact. Be prepared for their mood shifts. Continue to be kind, loving, and respectful. They won't forget your consideration and will find a way to repay you.

Indifferent profs, as described by Monte, are cold, aloof, apathetic, and cynical. They hate teaching and see it more as a job than a vocation. Intimacy for them provokes anxiety. They see learning as a detached interaction with neutral subject matter.

Don't imitate indifferent professors' coolness toward the subject matter. Remember that the messenger is not equal to the message. Throw yourself into the readings to derive some real warmth from the subject area. If possible, switch courses.

Obsessive profs are order and neatness freaks. They need organization, control, and exactness in every detail of the class. Their fanaticism about details, rigidity, and inflexibility both anger and numb students.

It is important to follow the rules of obsessive professors. Be sure you always come to class and do so *promptly*. Meet their due dates. When you are confused about requirements, always ask for clarification. Avoid these teachers in the future.

To Pledge or Not to Pledge

This above all: to thine own self be true.
—Polonius in Shakespeare's Hamlet

"To go Greek or not . . . ?" that is the question. It won't take long before you must decide whether or not to pledge a fraternity or sorority. This decision will greatly affect the quality of your entire college experience. Make it carefully, only after weighing all the pros and cons.

There are three main types of these student associations. *Professional* fraternities and sororities are open by invitation to students and faculty in a particular field of study, for example, law, journalism, or engineering. *Honor* societies are for distinguished scholars of outstanding character who live up to other requirements established by the particular association. The most distinguished honor society is Phi Beta Kappa.

Social fraternities and sororities, where membership is by invitation, promote the social purposes of their members. To join one of these involves a screening process called "rushing," when you are approached or rushed by members about the possibility of joining. Rush Week typically takes place early in the spring term when a candidate visits the prospective fraternity or sorority houses. To receive a bid (acceptance into particular association) requires the vote of each member. Thus, potential pledges must spend considerable time during Rush Week getting to know the members of the most desirable houses. If a candidate receives a bid and accepts, then he or she becomes a pledge. Pledges typically have to endure an embarrassing initiation rite which could involve controversial hazings, some of which have led to injury and even death for new pledges. These initiation rites and the hazings associated with them have given some fraternities a bad press in recent years.

Benefits of Membership

Why do college students join fraternities and sororities? The most common reason members give is instant camaraderie. Being a member of a Greek letter association promises members a new set of friends, a sense of belonging to a brotherhood or sisterhood, and an instantaneous social life. Academic fringe benefits include advice from older members concerning courses and profs, and access to a bank of books, old course notes, exams, quizzes, term papers, and projects that can help the member survive college. Of course, drawing on these resources often borders on outright cheating.

Today, an increasing number of Greek societies are attempting to fight the "Animal House" image, the perception that the organization's only purpose is to throw the best party on campus. Most fraternities and sororities participate in various service projects which foster a sense of community while tapping into the idealism and goodness of college students who want to make a positive contribution in the service of others.

Drawbacks of Membership

A negative of joining a Greek letter society is that you might push away non-brothers or non-sisters from your circle of friends. In addition, you must be willing to make an enormous commitment of time and energy for the various activities of the brotherhood or sisterhood. Also, there are initiation fees and dues for membership, at least several hundred dollars each year.

Too much partying, a tradition of hazing, and being a member of a closed society—all these contribute to the negative stereotyping of some Greek societies. In addition, Greek brothers and sisters need to conform to the traditions, customs, and expectations of the group, thus surrendering a certain amount of individuality in the process.

Some of these negative generalizations may be more or less pronounced for a given fraternity or sorority on your campus. If you are even remotely considering joining a fraternity or sorority, be sure to answer for yourself or inquire of others the answers to these questions:

▸ Do you have the same interests as a good majority of the fraternity or sorority members in question?

▸ What is the GPA of the members? (Hanging around with good students is bound to have a positive effect.)

▸ How much are the annual dues? Can you afford them?

▸ How much time must you devote to your Greek brothers or sisters? Will the time and other commitments distract you from the main purpose of college—getting an education?

▸ Are positive things going on with this association? How will membership in it make you a better person?

▸ What are the living conditions at the house, especially for new pledges? What is the food like?

▸ What is the purpose of the initiation? Is it dehumanizing or is it just harmless fun?

▸ Is this something you really want to do, or are you being "rushed" into it?

Recommendation: The first year of college is a time of adjustment. If you have an intense desire to join a Greek letter society, spend your first year studying the various options to be sure you find one that is worthy of your own high values. Wait until the spring term of your sophomore year before you agree to pledge.

Dating, Love, and Sex

So live that you wouldn't be ashamed
to sell the family parrot to the town gossip.

—Will Rogers

A real advantage to college life is the opportunity to develop, nurture, and cherish mature friendships with all kinds of people of both genders. This may be an eye-opener for you, especially if you attended an all-boy or all-girl high school or if you were very shy around the opposite sex during your high-school years.

In college, make it a top priority to develop opposite-sex friendships built on equality, mutual respect, and open communication. A big step to poise and adult maturity is the ability to relate in friendship to the other half of the human race. Seize every opportunity to converse with members of the other sex by chatting before class, eating meals together in mixed groups, joining study groups, participating in an extracurricular activity, attending concerts and movies, and dating.

Make Friends First

A good rule of thumb is to make friends first with members of the opposite sex before you begin any "serious" dating. You will, of course, want to date in college, and you should when the opportunity presents itself. However, the nature of dating in contemporary society too quickly narrows the field and closes you off to other opposite-sex friendships. Note the contrast: friendship includes others; dating tends to be exclusive. Friendship is open and public; dating leans toward togetherness and privacy. Friendship is social and interpersonal while avoiding the trappings and pitfalls of romance; dating can move closer and closer to self-absorption, possessiveness, and jealousy. C. S. Lewis observed in *The Four Loves*, "Lovers are normally face to face, absorbed in each other; friends, side by side, absorbed in some common interest."

Meeting and befriending members of the opposite sex as equals is freeing. It liberates the male especially from the societal stereotype of the individual conqueror who wins by dominating women. And having friendships with men can remind women that they are persons deserving of profound respect, not because of their external appearance, but because they possess inner beauty and worth as God's creation.

Dating Tips

For some young men and women, the freshman year of college will be their first opportunity to date. Others will have the experience of previous dating, but now they have the advantage of no one knowing their high-school background with its failures and successes. As you begin your college career, resolve to meet and date a variety of people. It is good "to play the field," even if you have left a boyfriend or girlfriend behind. (Recall that it is not a good idea to promise that you won't even meet and interact with a variety of people of the opposite sex while at college, let alone date others.) Befriending and dating many people will help you to widen your experiences and grow as a person.

Make sure to show a genuine interest in your dates. Engage in meaningful conversation. Ask about everything from their families and academic majors to their likes and dislikes.

Build your dating relationships on openness and honesty. If someone is going to fall in love with you, you want to make sure he or she knows the real you. This means being up-front about your religious and ethical values. Ideally, you will attract and find attractive a person whose moral standards and religious beliefs support and nurture your own, for example, someone who is:

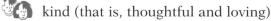 kind (that is, thoughtful and loving)

 honest

 intelligent

 loyal

considerate (concerned about you and your interests)

interesting (multidimensional)

 empathetic

 affectionate (open to giving and receiving compliments; warm)

 possessing of a sense of humor

principled (a person of integrity)

Find these qualities in a potential dating companion and you will have found someone who is bound to make you a better person.

Sex Facts

To state the obvious, we live in a sex-saturated world. Note the following news reports of interest to college students:

- A *Glamour* magazine article reported the results of a Kinsey Institute survey of college students' sexual practices. In the group surveyed, 80 percent of the men and 73 percent of the women had had sexual intercourse. On average, the men had slept with eight different partners and the women six. Sixty-two percent had not used a condom the last time they had intercourse. Nearly one-third of the sexually active women had caught an STD. And, of the 600 midwestern university students surveyed, 80 percent considered themselves "moderate" or "conservative" rather than "liberal."[3]

- A recent *New York Times* leading article reported how regular HIV testing of college students is becoming more and more common.

- More than one million teens get pregnant each year in America. Close to half these pregnancies end in abortion.

- Nearly half of sexually active young people do not use any contraceptive devices at the time of their first sexual encounter. "Substantial" numbers do not do so later.[4]

Your College and Sex

In general, don't look for your college to take the role of your parents in monitoring your sexual behavior. The vast majority of colleges today shrink from any responsibility of trying to control the sex lives of undergraduates. Freshman orientation may include sessions on date rape, alcohol abuse, and "safe sex," but there is little attempt subsequently to monitor what students do on their own time. Coed dorms, few if any rules about after-hours room visitation, and the lack of a curfew all convey the message that students are on their own when managing their sexual behavior.

College students are at an age when their sex drives are at their peaks or near peaks. With all the beautiful young people on campus, it is not unusual to have sex on the mind a good deal of the time. Sexual thoughts are natural and normal. They only are wrong when they become lustful, that is deliberately inflaming your desires past the boundaries God has set for healthy and moral sexual attraction. Also, having sexual thoughts and feelings does not mean a person *must* act on them. Of course, today's popular society assumes that you will, that you cannot resist your sexual urges. Colleges often convey this same message, for example, by placing condom machines in dorm restrooms.

Your classmates and dormmates will have various thoughts about premarital sex. Some of them have decided to abstain from sex until marriage. Others are confused, undecided, and wavering. Still others are sexually active with one partner or promiscuously active with many partners.

You will hear many reasons for why you should be having sex; among the most prevalent is that it is the "cool" thing to be doing. Your sexual orientation or level of maturity may be questioned if you aren't having sex. The reality is that freedom from parental rules + raging hormones + the message that sexual experience before marriage is inevitable + many peers who habitually and without question indulge in sex all add up to powerful temptations to engage in sex in college.

Sexual Intercourse Is for Marriage

Undoubtedly you know quite well the Christian teaching on full sexual sharing: sexual intercourse is a profound form of communication filled with deep meaning. Sexual intercourse is a body-language that signifies the love of one spouse for the other in a total gift of self. It says: "I am giving you my entire self, completely and exclusively. Through this act, I declare my total and lasting commitment to you."

True love and lasting commitment are the bottom-line reasons why sexual intercourse is to be reserved for marriage. In marriage, a couple has publicly promised exclusive and mutual self-giving "for better or for worse, in sickness and in health" as long as both shall live. This unbreakable promise creates a stable relationship that can nourish the couple's love and provide the proper context for the raising of children. There is no way for this promise to be made (and kept) between a man and woman outside of marriage.

To use the language of married love outside marriage is a travesty. Sexual lovemaking should speak the language of full commitment. The unmarried couple, though, can always bail out of their relationship with "no strings attached."

The church promotes saving sex until marriage because sexual intercourse symbolizes and expresses the permanent commitment of true love. Couples who invoke the word "love" in their premarital sexual unions are deceiving themselves. Psychology shows that sexual intimacy before marriage is all too often a front for manipulation, possessiveness, anger, escape, and a host of other emotional problems. Broken relationships always cause hurt. And misusing sexual intercourse is a source of great emotional and spiritual hurt when the relationship ends.

What unmarried men and women need in their relationship is premarital *love*. Remember, St. Paul lists *patience* as the first quality of love (see 1 Corinthians 13). True love waits for marriage to have sex.

Benefits of Living Chastely

Christian teaching promotes chastity as a virtue which empowers everyone to control their sexual expression to conform to their state in life. Married people must abstain from sex with everyone but their spouse. A non-married college student must abstain from sexual intercourse until marriage. Living chastely is incredibly freeing, and it brings a host of benefits. For example:

- You will have a clear conscience and a right relationship with God.

- You will be disease-free. (Abstinence is 100 percent "safe sex." Despite media hype, there is no other form of safe sex. Living chastely will inoculate you from more than 50 STDs, including AIDS, which results in death.)

- You won't get pregnant or be responsible for a pregnancy. You won't have to consider abortion or a premature decision to marry.

- You will save yourself great anxiety and worry over the *possibilities* of catching a disease or having a baby. Worry makes you neglect your studies, thus endangering your academic career.

- You will treat yourself and others with respect.

- You will master the self-control that you will need in all aspects of life. Your future marriage will require discipline for you and your spouse to remain faithful through "thick and thin."

- You are free from playing sexual games. As a result, you can redirect your positive sexual energy to worthwhile pursuits like sports and various service projects.

- You will make a positive countercultural statement about chastity and abstinence to refute today's conventional wisdom that reduces humans to sexual

animals or programmed machines. You will witness to the dignity of persons as free, loving, and intelligent beings who *can* control themselves.

▸ You will have the time and freedom to build true friendships. Lasting marriages are built on friendship. Sex is only a part of marriage, albeit a very good part. A chaste lifestyle will free you to find a potential mate who is like-minded and willing to accept you for the person you are.

How to Handle and Avoid Sexual Temptations

Remaining chaste and abstaining from sexual relations during your years in college requires making that decision for yourself right now. It is a decision that includes these actions:

1. *Stay close to Jesus.* Unless you are an angel (a spirit without a body), you will need Jesus' help to master sexual temptations. Jesus calls us to high standards. To follow him is often difficult, but he promised that he would help his friends. Ask for

God's help in this area, both in private prayer and in the weekly eucharistic liturgy.

2. *Choose like-minded friends.* We all need a support group that will nurture, not undermine, our values.

3. *Be sure your date knows your standards.* No one has the right to demand sex because money was spent on you or time together was shared. Say "no" firmly and strongly if your date begins to pressure you for sex. You are not compelled to share your reasons for saying "no."

4. *Know where to draw the line.* Drawing the line means staying sober. Drugs and alcohol lower inhibitions and resolve. Alcohol abuse is implicated in many date rapes.

   Drawing the line means avoiding tempting situations. Sex is beautiful, exciting, passionate, and progressive. Once sexual passion kicks into gear, it yearns for greater intimacy and union. Avoid places that will lower your resolve, for example, the back seat of a car or being alone together in a dorm room.

   Drawing the line means dressing modestly. You don't want to send the wrong message.

   Drawing the line means properly handling displays of affection. For example, prolonged open-mouthed kissing and petting comprise the slippery slope to the full sexual expression of intercourse. Limit your show of affection to hand holding, hugs, and light kissing.

   Drawing the line means avoiding sexually suggestive movies and conversations. These can enflame sexual desires and lead to improper behavior.

   Remember, the feeling of *wanting* to have sex does not mean you have to have sex. As a free human being, you can control your behavior.

To Party or Not

Let us strip off anything that slows us down
or holds us back, and especially those sins
that wrap themselves so tightly around our feet
and trip us up; and let us run with patience
the particular race that God has set before us.

—Hebrews 12:1 (TLB)

In the minds of many, college students and partying are synonymous. The enduring popularity of a film like *Animal House* which extols partying and drinking into oblivion perpetuates the myth that college years are primarily for getting drunk or getting high. Unfortunately, some students, including many college freshmen, live that myth. The consequences can be tragic.

"Binge drinking" is a particular problem. A binge drinker is defined as someone who has had five to six drinks at one sitting within the previous two weeks. A study in the *Journal of the American Medical Association* reported that of 17,592 college students surveyed at 140 four-year colleges, 44 percent were binge drinkers.[5] The study also noted that binge drinkers were seven to ten times more likely than non-binge drinkers not to use protection when having sex, to engage in unplanned sex, to get in trouble with the campus police, to damage property, and to get hurt or injured. Binge drinkers reported significantly higher frequencies of dangerous driving habits after drinking.

A Harvard School of Public Health study reported that one-third of college freshmen join in binge drinking, when it is popular on campus, *before* attending their first class.[6]

Setting Limits

Inebriation is wrong because it dehumanizes. It diminishes or destroys one's capacity to think rationally. It lessens or extinguishes will power. People who drink beyond the point of control typically get physically sick. In addition, they often get morally ill, causing harm to themselves and others. Christians recognize that immoderate use of alcohol and recreational experimentation with drugs destroy the dignity of a person.

Decide ahead of time what you are going to do about partying with alcohol and other drugs. Your advanced decision is the ounce of prevention you'll need to inoculate yourself against the temptations of peer pressure. Be proactive. Draw the line now. Here are some related guidelines to consider:

- ▶ Avoid chemicals as a way to deal with stress. Never begin using them; not even once. If you are dealing with an issue you cannot handle, go to the student life center or the Newman center chaplain and ask for help.

- ▶ Don't allow others to pressure you. Avoid high-pressure situations where it is a "manly" thing to drink as much and as quickly as possible. If you must drink, nurse a drink over a long period of time.

- ▶ If you want to do drugs, then leave college! Ask yourself: Do you know anyone who is a better student because he or she is on drugs? Are any better problem-solvers because of their addiction to drugs? Papers written while high that seem creative at first are mostly nonsensical or disjointed when the drugs wear off.

- ▶ If you must drink, devise a buddy system where another person looks out for you (and you for the other person). Know your limit. Know your partner's limit.

- ▶ If you or any friends will be going to or from a party in a car, *always* have a designated driver. You are socially irresponsible and deviant if you don't follow this most basic rule. You also have a death wish or prison wish for yourself or others. Yes, countless college students die in alcohol-related car accidents. Yes, many college students—when driving while intoxicated—kill and maim innocent people.

- ▶ If your roommate is doing drugs, speak up and show him or her where to get help. If this doesn't work, talk to your RA. If you get no satisfaction, change room-mates as soon as possible. People on drugs are dangerous to themselves and others. At the least, he or she will bring down your academic performance and social possibilities.

- ▸ If you are under age, consider the question of how you are going to break the law to obtain liquor. Will you have to lie (false ID) to do so? What policy, if any, does your college have if you get caught breaking the law? Consider: Is drinking *that* important to you?

- ▸ Be your own person. Some things are wrong. Can you stand up to peer pressure? Will you?

- ▸ *Never* drink anything from a punch bowl. You don't know what is in the concoction or what has been added to the mix.

- ▸ Do you find vomiting and passing out attractive? This is one of the common results of binge drinking, especially among underage drinkers.

- ▸ Out-of-control drinkers are classified as alcoholics. Is this the label you want for yourself?

- ▸ If you are taking any kind of medication, don't drink. The combination could be lethal.

- ▸ If you are drinking all the time, you have a problem. Get help now before it ruins your college career and your life.

- ▸ Moderation in everything!

We can all tell stories about how the abuse of alcohol in college has ruined lives. I personally know of former students who drowned or died in car accidents after college-drinking episodes. I know one young man who went to prison for sexual assault while intoxicated. I know a student who, when drunk, fell down a stairwell. He is permanently disabled today. I know another who contracted HIV because of his promiscuous sexual behavior while under the influence of alcohol.

The most common fallout among my former students, however, has been the literally hundreds who were not able to handle the newfound freedom of the first year of college. "Free at last," they let loose with the drinking and began to party almost constantly. The results were very predictable: flunking out of college either after the first semester or most certainly by the end of the first year. Then, if they're lucky, they go off to a junior college to get back on track. Maybe after a year, they enroll at a state college near to home. Most never make it back to their dream college. There is good news, however. All 26 fraternities and sororities at the University of Colorado recently voted to ban alcohol from all gatherings held in chapter houses. Drunken party animals are now defined at Colorado as "social misfits."[7] As you enter college, consider carefully how the use, misuse, or nonuse of alcohol and drugs will define who you are.

What About Cheating?

I care not what others think of what I do, but I care very much about what I think I do. That is character.
— Theodore Roosevelt

The Chronicle of Higher Education reports that two-thirds of college students admit to cheating on tests.[8] When I shared this statistic with my graduating high-school seniors they were surprised that the figure was so low. My students were on to something. A psychology professor later surveyed 3,000 college students from around the country. Again, two-thirds admitted to cheating on tests in high school. He was disturbed not only by the high numbers, but their attitudes. Those who cheated said they felt no remorse for their actions.[9]

Students cheat for several reasons. Most who cheat have low self-esteem. They cave into the pressure to get good grades by taking the easy way out, even knowing what they are doing is morally wrong. They cheat because everyone else cheats. They cheat because they are lazy.[10]

Not too long ago a college student wrote a popular book

entitled *Cheating 101: The Benefits and Fundamentals of Earning an Easy "A."* The primer revealed tactics of how a group of friends can work together to cheat on multiple-choice exams. Many college students seem to treat cheating as a game in which you win as long as you don't get caught. Or, they rationalize cheating as balanced by the honest work they do in school. They forget that even one incident of cheating brands them as a cheater.

Before long, you'll notice advertisements in various publications (maybe even your college newspaper) targeted to college students for "research services." In short, for a price, you can buy a term paper on any topic. There is apparently a brisk market for ghost-written college term papers because the "business" continues to thrive. These companies maintain their papers are only to aid a student's "research" and are not to be used as a final work. But many students do turn these bought papers in for a grade. Buyer beware: most college professors are on to this scam. They are easily able to recognize these "professionally" written papers. If you decide to go this route, know the consequences. If you are found out, you will merit a certain failure on the paper or class, and possibly severe penalties from the school, up to expulsion.

Temptations to cheat, as well as to plagiarize (that is, to pass off another's work as your own), will meet you at every turn throughout your college career. Remember the advice of a college mathematics professor who said to his class:

> Today, I am giving two exams: one in calculus, the other in honesty. My hope is that you will pass both. If you are going to fail one, fail calculus. There are many good people in the world who are lost solving calc problems. But there are no good people in the world who cannot pass the test of honesty.

Personal integrity is the touchstone of character. It is in short supply today. As a Christian, your commitment to simple, basic honesty will be a resounding witness to your peers. In the words of Alexander Pope, "An honest person is the noblest work of God."

Five
KEEPING PHYSICALLY AND SPIRITUALLY FIT

The Sea of Galilee and the Dead Sea each have the same water source flowing down from Mount Hermon. Yet these bodies of water are markedly different.

Because it has several river outlets, the Sea of Galilee is able to maintain its freshness. The Sea of Galilee teems with aquatic life. Additionally, it gives life by irrigating the surrounding Jordan Plain.

The Dead Sea has no river outlets. Evaporation in the desert heat quickly carries away the fresh water that flows into it. The brine content of the Dead Sea is nearly six times that of the oceans. There is nothing living in the Dead Sea except a few kinds of microbes.

Compare yourself to these two types of bodies of water. If you have an outlet in the form of a generous heart, healthy eating and living patterns, a solid exercise program, and an active spiritual life, then you will thrive in body, mind, and spirit. However, if you grow listless, stout, and lazy by developing bad personal habits, you will become physically, psychologically, and spiritually stagnant.

This final chapter looks at ways to develop and maintain healthy habits and coping techniques for physical and spiritual fitness while you are in college. The Romans had an expression, *mens sana in corpore sano*, "a healthy mind in a healthy body." This ancient wisdom is worth adopting. It will help you to handle the rigors of a challenging academic life. Included in your plan should be an awareness and practice of:

- Healthy eating
- Sensible exercise
- Safety on campus
- Stress reduction
- Maintenance of spiritual health

Smart Eating

Dietary self-control is the capacity to
break a chocolate bar in half, smell its
heavenly aroma, and then eat just one piece.
—some good advice

College freshmen usually have a love-hate relationship with the cafeteria. They love it because it is a great place to meet friends, unwind, and socialize. Also, most food plans allow you to go back for unlimited quantities of food. At home, you may have been limited to one helping of dessert. Not at college! You will find that no one will mind if you have an enormous mound of ice cream at every meal.

On the other hand, the *quality* of food on most campuses rarely receives high marks. You might find the daily main course mediocre at best. I recall that by the second semester of my freshman year I found the cafeteria food barely edible. Lots of late-night burgers and pizzas somehow sustained me until I moved off campus and did my own cooking.

The problem with large quantities of food, readily available, and late-night eating is that they lead to the "famous freshman 15." Many frosh are surprised when they go home for Thanksgiving or Christmas break to discover that they have put on considerable weight, up to fifteen pounds. Clothes fit more tightly and that svelte, lean look from summer has quickly disappeared. When your mom makes a comment about your weight, you know it is time to take stock of your college-eating habits.

Bad eating habits are like a comfortable bed—easy to get into but hard to get out of. College is tough enough without lugging extra weight around. Start out with a plan for healthy eating and you will save yourself the struggle to lose unwanted pounds during the second semester. Consider the following tips for a healthy, balanced diet:

Eat three modest-sized meals each day.

Avoid the fast-and-binge cycle. Consuming three meals, even if one meal is light, dulls sudden hunger surges and spreads out your energy level during the day. Eat a variety of foods from the basic food groups: milk, meat, fruit/vegetable, and grain. Substitute as necessary; for example, if you are a vegetarian make sure to supplement with other non-meat protein items.

Always eat breakfast.

Like your mom says, "Breakfast is the most important meal." In the college cafeteria, breakfast may be the best-tasting meal. It's almost impossible to ruin bacon, eggs, and pancakes. However, you should plan to indulge in these greasy fares only once or twice a week. Also, avoid sugared cereals, donuts, and pastries. Too many sugary foods will cause an afternoon crash and the need for another sugar "fix" to get you through the day. Rather, eat cereal and toasted breads with fiber. Low-sugared jellies on low-fat bagels and muffins will satisfy your sweet tooth. Also make sure to stock up on Vitamin C. Eat plenty of fruit and drink fruit juices.

Veg out for lunch.

Your mother was also right when she told you vegetables are good for you. Plan to eat a salad for your midday meal. It's always a pain to eat salads when you have to cut up and wash the vegetables yourself. The beauty of salad bars is that the hard work is already done for you. Watch your fat intake by using a low-fat dressing. Supplement the salad with a cup of soup and a piece of whole wheat bread. Research shows that a high-protein versus a high-carbohydrate lunch increases afternoon alertness.

If you think you might miss lunch, carry along an extra piece of fruit, a bagel, or sandwich in your knapsack. If you completely go without eating in the afternoon, you're likely to overeat at dinner. Also, instead of a steady diet of sweetened soda pop, drink flavored mineral water, fruit juice, herbal tea, or just plain water. By the way, drinking eight glasses of water every day is not only healthy advice, it is a great way to keep you from overeating. Your stomach can only handle so much volume.

Eat sensibly at dinner.

Avoid fried foods, especially french fries. Eat grilled chicken and fish whenever possible. They are low in fat and cholesterol. Cut the fat away from other meats. Even if you have to force yourself, eat at least one serving of vegetables at every meal. Limit yourself to one dessert. The key at dinner time is to eat slowly, drink plenty of fluids, and resist the urge to go back for seconds.

Don't be a junk-food junkie.

Despite the presence of good, nutritional (but admittedly not always tasty) food on college campuses, fast food still rules the day for many students. Burgers, pizza, fries, tacos, and donuts *are* the meal plan for many college students seven days a week. It's okay to have fun and occasionally have a junk-food snack to break up a late-night study session; but always remember that those foods are high in fat and calories. Translation: extra weight, sluggishness, and potential health problems. If you know you'll be up late working on a term paper, stock your dorm refrigerator and shelves with some low-fat snacks (e.g., fruit, popcorn without butter, carrots).

Beware of eating disorders.

There is a big difference between dieting to maintain a healthy weight and dieting to achieve a weight perceived to be in line with advertised models or athletes. The obsession with thinness can lead to serious eating disorders which often end in health problems or death. Two common eating disorders that appear frequently on college campuses, especially among women, are anorexia nervosa and bulimia.

Anorexia nervosa is deliberate self-starvation caused by a fear of being fat. "Anorexia" means "without appetite." "Nervosa" means "of nervous origin." The disorder comes from a distorted body image and, for perfectionists, is often a psychological plea for love. Its major symptoms are a refusal to eat, except small portions, and a denial of hunger. Anorexia nervosa results in abnormal weight loss, hair loss, sensitivity to cold, and cessation of menstruation.

Bulimia involves rapidly consuming large amounts of food in a short period of time, and then vomiting after bingeing. Vomiting causes swollen salivary glands, broken blood vessels in the eyes, discolored teeth, irritation of the esophagus, and potassium depletion which leads to life-threatening heart attacks. Bulimia also involves the abuse of laxatives and diet and water pills. Bulimics are often perfectionists. One study reports that more than four in ten first-year college women would consider bulimia to lose weight.

If you notice a roommate or friend with any symptoms of these eating disorders, point them out to your RA. These are psychological conditions that can be treated.

Sensible Exercise

Whether you think you can or think you can't,
you're right.
—Henry Ford

Besides a healthy diet, you should commit yourself to a regular exercise program in college. After college, few people have to train to play competitive sports. The college years are the time to develop an exercise and sports plan that will carry you throughout life.

The secret formula for an effective exercise program is to progress slowly, getting the body gradually ready for exercise. Walking across campus versus riding the campus shuttle service is a good way to start! You can later "graduate" to power walks, jogging, running, or bicycling.

Also, most colleges have athletic and recreational facilities on par with most private health clubs. Spiking a volleyball, playing a hard-fought game of handball or racquetball, swimming a half-mile on a regular basis, lifting weights, or working out on the various exercise paraphernalia not only keeps your body in tip-top shape, it is also a great way to relieve stress (more on stress to follow).

Another option, especially when you determine you have the academics under control, is to participate in an intramural sport. You will likely find a variety of intramural sports in college, everything from the basics like basketball and soccer to more unusual entries like coed water polo played in an inner tube! Many college students enjoy participating in intramural sports not only for the inherent value of the exercise, but for the competition, companionship, and the break in the routine.

If you are not into sports, you don't have to force yourself to be miserable just because you think you have to develop into an athlete. Why add more stress to your life? As long as you do some exercise—walking, cycling, throwing a Frisbee—it is okay to enjoy sports as a spectator. You can even ignore athletics altogether.

But *do* plan to do some exercise on a daily basis. Just like other busy people, you have to commit yourself to it, no matter how filled your schedule. Remember, your mind *will* function better in a well-tuned, healthy body.

Safety Consciousness

An ounce of prevention is worth a pound of cure
—a famous saying

Campus crime is a problem. You ignore it at your peril. One out of three college students becomes a victim of crime, usually of a crime committed by another student and usually involving alcohol. In fact alcohol may be a factor in as many as 90 percent of violent campus crimes. In most of these cases both the victim and the perpetrator have been drinking.[1]

Since 1990, when the federal Student Right-to-Know and Campus Security Act became law, you can more easily find the crime statistics for your college. Inquire with the campus security or police for their recent statistics. Murder, rape, robbery, aggravated assault, burglary, and auto theft do take place on and around college campuses. You need to be aware of this reality and use common sense to prevent becoming a victim. But you also need to know that most campuses are far safer than the downtown areas of major cities and their suburbs. Also, campuses are typically safer than their surrounding areas as well.

Take the time to develop a safety plan and safety awareness. Here are some points for consideration:

Be sure to attend freshmen orientation to gain information about safety procedures on campus. On your tour of the campus, note the location of emergency phones. Learn how to contact campus security. Also, carry with you the appropriate emergency phone numbers other than 911 (e. g, RA, infirmary, counseling center).

🔓 Travel in groups when walking across campus, especially at night or early morning. Walking alone at night—especially for women—is dangerous. Use the campus escort service, a group of paid students or volunteers who will meet you where you are and walk with you where you need to go. Always walk in well-lit areas. Be aware of your surroundings. Carry your keys in your hand so you can quickly enter your car, dorm, or apartment.

🔓 Don't jog alone, especially off campus. When you plan to go off campus, let your roommate or a friend know your plans and when you expect to be back.

🔓 Property theft is by far the most common campus crime. Leave irreplaceable valuables at home. Engrave your initials on expensive items that you do bring to school, like your computer and bike. Remember, always lock your dorm door. If you are a commuter, always lock your car. It takes only eight seconds to enter a room or car and take something. Never leave your backpack unattended. Your wallet, portable CD player, calculator, texts, and other belongings can instantly disappear.

🔓 Beware of developing a false sense of security. For example, do not disconnect alarms, prop open residence hall doors, or allow strangers entrance to your dorm. Double check to see that you lock your door and windows at night. It is your right to have broken locks or windows repaired immediately.

🔓 Report strangers roaming around in your dorm.

🔓 Never drive with someone who was drinking. Avoid alcohol yourself; too much of it impairs judgment. It also makes some students violent. You can often trace date rape and assaults to inebriated students.

🔓 Be alert in elevators.

🔓 Exercise caution when making new friends. Don't bring strangers back to your dorm room. Date in groups until you get to know well the person you are dating. College campuses have a higher incidence of rape than some major U. S. cities. One in four college women will be victimized by rapes or attempted rapes. More than half of college women know a rape victim. Freshman women have the highest percentage of rapes, most frequently occurring in their first three weeks at school. The most likely rapists at college are sexually aggressive male friends.

When you date, go to public places. Let your date know your standards and limits concerning alcohol and sex. Take some money along for a cab ride back to school in case your date gets obnoxious and dangerous.

Report all crimes or attempted crimes. If you are raped, seek medical help immediately. Involve relatives and close friends for psychological support.

Coping with Stress

> The only people with no problems are dead.
>
> —some practical advice

Stress is defined as "physical, mental, or emotional strain or tension." Not all stress is bad, though a number of diseases and illnesses including heart disease, high blood pressure, and headaches are thought to be stress-related. The short of it is that stress is an inevitable part of human life. As the quote above expresses, with no stress we would be dead. To stay physically, psychologically, and mentally fit in college, an important key is knowing how to manage stress.

Identifying Stressors and Managing Stress

A good starting point in stress management is to locate the sources of negative stress that impede your performance. The following are typical stress producers for the average college student:

- ▸ test-taking
- ▸ paper-writing
- ▸ selecting courses

- homesickness (especially true for freshmen)
- having an obnoxious roommate
- meeting parental expectations about grades and college major
- the lack of money
- the lack of sleep (eight hours per night are needed)
- being ill
- experiencing social pressure from friends and the demands of extracurricular activities
- having a job that chops away at study time
- being involved in a romantic relationship (or lack thereof)
- dealing with unfair professors
- carrying unrealistic self expectations

Merely naming what is stressing you can be a great help in reducing its negative influence. For example, when you know that your fear of oral reports causes you stress, you can tackle this problem directly. Practice public speaking regularly by contributing to class discussions. If your course load of 20 units is unmanageable, find relief by dropping a course or two. Or, if scheduling courses stretches you to the limit, be sure to have a couple of contingency plans with alternative classes at registration time.

Here are other strategies for stress reduction and management:

Exercise vigorously. Physical activity correlates well with mental acuity and psychological well being.

Eat well. If you are run down physically, you'll lack the stamina to cope with stressors.

Prioritize. List what is really important. Do the items on the top of the list first. Eliminate as many nonessentials as possible.

Relax. Listen to music. Take naps. Shop. Take in a movie. Golf. Allow yourself frequent breaks from study, for example, by enjoying an occasional bull session with friends or dormmates.

 Distinguish between working hard and being a workaholic. Hard workers are organized and focused so they can accomplish many things. But they know when to stop and have a life other than work (study). Workaholics are disorganized, escape their problems through work, don't know when or how to relax, and are one-dimensional, that is, unable to converse about more than one topic.

Serve others. Jesus taught that if you lose yourself in serving others, you'll find yourself. Participate in a college-sponsored effort that aids the less fortunate.

Accept your humanity. If much of your stress is self-induced ("I have to get all A's"), perhaps you are being unrealistic. Set realistic goals for yourself.

Get help. Maintain a support group of friends or family and, as needed, school counselors and health professionals. Talking problems out is an effective stress reducer.

Pray. More information on prayer to follow.

Depression and Suicide

Mild depression hits everyone, even college students. With so many demands placed on one's time and energy, it is natural on occasion to feel sad, discouraged, and "burned out." These feelings may lead to sleeplessness, energy and appetite loss, anxiety, and feelings of emptiness. These symptoms may be more acute if a major stressor occurs: a death in your family, your parents divorce, or a serious illness strikes a friend.

Realize that temporary depression is very natural. To reduce it, use some of the stress management techniques covered in this chapter. Never use alcohol or drugs to "drown your sorrows." They, in fact, will weaken your resolve to improve your outlook and will make you more vulnerable to negative thoughts.

When depression lasts over a longer period of time it can indicate a more serious problem. It can even lead to thoughts of suicide. One study found that 70 percent of college students contemplated suicide. The three major reasons for doing so were (1) intense pressure to achieve high grades, (2) social isolation, and (3) a perceived failure to win parental love.

If you notice any of the following suicide warning signs in yourself, a friend, or a roommate, speak up and seek help. Parents, friends, college chaplains, and Suicide Prevention Agencies *will* help you or a friend get through the tough times.

Suicide Warning Signs

- A notable change in eating and sleeping patterns
- Withdrawal from friends, family, and school groups
- Persistent boredom
- A decline in academic performance
- Unusually violent or rebellious behavior
- Drug or alcohol abuse
- An unusual neglect of personal appearance
- Difficulty in concentration
- A radical change in personality
- Psychosomatic complaints[2]

Maintaining Spiritual Health

Listen! I am sending you out
just like sheep to a pack of wolves.
You must be as cautious as snakes
and as gentle as doves. Watch out.

—Matthew 10:16-17a (TEV)

Medical science tells that five nutrients—proteins, carbohydrates, fats, vitamins, and minerals—are needed for nutritional health and growth. Neglect any of these and your body will pay the price. The case is similar with spiritual health and growth.

Neglect any of five major spiritual nutrients—prayer, worship, community, service, and witness—and your soul will begin to suffer.

Prayer

Interestingly, 94 percent of Americans claim they believe in God, but 96 percent report that they pray![3] Figure that one out! Perhaps it has something to do with the truism, "There are no atheists in a foxhole." People naturally turn to God in prayer, even when they say they don't believe in God.

To be sure, college students pray, especially around test time! But prayer is most valuable when it is a way of life, not just a case of an emergency. Make prayer part of your daily routine as a student and you will reap great rewards. John Wesley, the father of Methodism and a great preacher, lived a strenuous, action-filled life. He once said, "Today, I have such a busy day before me that I cannot get through it with less than two hours of prayer."

Obviously, spending two hours each day in prayer would be impractical, if not impossible, for a studious collegian. But what about 15 minutes of daily prayer? The payoff is great. Pray regularly and you will . . .

. . . *gain a greater sense of self worth.* In prayer, you lift your mind and heart to God. When you do this, you will discover anew God's love and acceptance of *you* and come to appreciate more your tremendous worth as a person.

. . . *change for the better.* In prayer, God will fill your heart, mind, and soul, helping you to become a more virtuous person.

. . . *increase your energy.* Pope John Paul II is the most traveled pope in history and a man of boundless energy whose impact on twentieth-century history is incalculable. His source of strength is a day begun with prayer. Prayer will give you the strength to complete well the tasks of your day.

. . . *discover healing and an increase in happiness.* In prayer, God can touch and cure your emotional hurts. God forgives your sins. Through prayer you can come to a deeper realization that God is the source of true happiness, not the false gods of popularity, pettiness, prestige, or possessions.

. . . *solve some of your problems*. Students worry needlessly about many things. Prayer helps you center and gain insight on how to live your life constructively as a student. To quote a popular phrase, prayer can help you "let go and let God."

A first step in *prayer basics* is to make a regular time for prayer, for example in the morning in the break time between two classes, or right after dinner before hitting the books. The time just before going to sleep is also a good time to schedule fifteen minutes of prayer.

Next, find a special place for prayer where there will be limited distractions. Some possibilities are your dorm room (when your roomie is in class), the school chapel, or a remote sofa or chair in the library. When the weather is pleasant, you can pray outdoors on a bench or while walking to a favorite locale on or near campus.

Third, use some deep breathing exercises and relaxation techniques to help you calm down. Let the hyperactivity of your day drain out of your body. There is a direct relationship between a calm body and a calm spirit. You will soon discover that a relaxing prayer time each day is a great stress reducer.

There are countless ways to pray. For example, you can read a scripture text and apply the biblical insights to your life. Or, you may find reading a book on spirituality a helpful way to focus on your relationship with God.

No matter which way you choose, I recommend that you make personal conversation with Jesus a part of your prayer experience. Become aware of Jesus' presence in your life and his care for you. Know that Jesus is your friend. Talk to him as you would your best friend about your fears, your needs, your desires. Ask him for his forgiveness for your sins, your inattentiveness, your failures to love. Thank him for the gifts of health, friendship, family, and your abilities to do well in school.

Then, listen to Jesus. Recall the events of your past day—the people, the successes and failures, the dreams that came true and those that didn't. Ask for insight as to their meaning. Reflect on what God might be telling you through these people and events. Listen carefully to your heart. God will tell you *something*. It's up to you to listen!

Conclude your time with the Lord with a short resolution based on your insights. For example, you might resolve to strike up a conversation with a lonely classmate. You might promise to avoid alcohol. You might pledge to call or write a younger brother or sister at home.

Make prayer a part of your college life and you will be a happier, more fulfilled student.

Worship

A survey at Brown University found that 70 percent of students of all religions made an effort to attend church services while living with their parents. However, only 23 percent of the same students attended church while living at Brown.[4] If your parents practice their faith, one of their major concerns may be that you will stop going to church when you are at college.

I teach at a Catholic high school. When I ask my former students why they stop going to Mass at college, they offer many excuses: lack of time, "Mass is boring," laziness, fear of ridicule from dormmates who don't go, a bad experience with a church figure, or a problem with a given church teaching. Often the real reason is that the church represents an objective morality of right and wrong. And lax students, engaged in immoral activity like premarital sex or hedonistic drinking, do not want an authority figure like the church to challenge their newfound freedom and lifestyle.

College students also often adopt a noncommittal wariness toward the religion of their childhood. They see the college years as a time to sort out their goals, aspirations, beliefs; a time to figure out who they are, where they come from and where they are going, and the meaning of existence. The college years are rightfully a time for this type of deep questioning. Nevertheless, sincere questioning is not an isolated affair. The search for the meaning of life is best begun by acknowledging a higher power, God, and seeking ways to pay respect, to honor, and to worship God in the presence of other like-minded students.

A popular myth is that because the teachings of traditional religions seem so out of step with today's secular society, religion is dead on college campuses. Not true! In fact, the countercultural teachings of Christ have a strong appeal to sincere college students who are honestly searching for truth amid the cacophony of voices vying for their attention. For example, a survey of campus ministers around the country revealed that many Catholic students want to examine the church's spiritual heritage to make sense of their own lives in a secular world that is both amoral and immoral.[5]

Many college students do attend worship services. In fact, Mass attendance among Catholic college students is often higher than among the general population in regular Catholic parishes.[6]

Why do these college students continue to practice their faith? I suppose some Catholic students attend Mass out of habit, but most go simply to pray in the manner they have learned to be life-giving. They go to church to find support and companionship. They go to hear the challenge of God's word. They go for the orderly ritual which is very appealing when liturgy is done well. They may even go for that good feeling of doing the right thing by worshipping God for one hour in return for the other 167 hours the Creator has given them. They go to receive the Lord Jesus himself.

I would guess that Christian students of other denominations would express similar reasons for attending Sunday worship services.

Search, examine your beliefs, ask fundamental questions. But remember that these worthwhile college activities do *not* exclude worshipping with other Christian seekers gathered around the table of faith.

Community

When describing today's college scene, Michael J. Buckley paraphrases the "death-of-God" philosopher, Friderich Nietzsche: "What are these universities now if not tombs of God—monuments to the death of God within our academic culture?"[7] One thing is for sure, at some time during your college years, someone will belittle, challenge, or attack your religious beliefs. My former students and my own children have told me about attacks against their Catholic faith.

You may face mean-spirited opposition from many sources, including professors. Perhaps you will have an instructor like the one my daughter had who told her that "thinking" people cannot possibly accept the resurrection of Jesus Christ, the most precious truth for Christians. Or maybe you will meet other professors who will belittle the church's pro-life views. You will surely discover a secular mindset among some professors and administrators (even at Catholic or other Christian colleges) who are overtly hostile to traditional religion, especially Catholicism. This should neither surprise nor shock you since many of them have rejected absolute truth. The church, which represents an objective morality that teaches the existence of truth independent of one's opinion, is a threat to their comfortable, "value-free" system of education.

When your classmates notice you practicing your religion, you will probably find yourself engaged in some heated and "heavy" conversations with them as well. Many people, including those who are your age, have absorbed the conventional morality of the day that holds that all values are simply a matter of taste. They have concluded that morality is simply a matter of "anything goes for you as long as it does not affect me." They might ridicule the Christ-inspired teaching that certain behaviors are wrong despite the circumstances or a person's intentions. Don't be surprised if you find little peer support on issues like the evil of abortion or the value of self-control in matters relating to sex.

You may even be pressured by classmates who do practice their religion. For example, Catholics often feel intimidated by fundamentalist Christians who know the scriptures extremely well and quote them liberally. Some Christians belong to churches that have a strong evangelical outreach and may even try to convert you to their particular denomination.

Also, you might come in contact with one or more of the 2,500-plus religious cults in operation today. They often prey on lonely, depressed, and stressed-out people who are your age. Cult recruiters sometimes hang around college counseling centers or cafeterias looking for students who seem isolated. Cults have a strong appeal to middle-class youths who are vulnerable and susceptible to the techniques of instant friendship, community acceptance, and the giving of out-of-proportion attention called "love bombing." Once an initiate has been hooked, the cult leaders try to get the new member to cut ties with friends and family. Though cults are not the threat on campus today that they were once, they still are present.

In general, your best strategy for coping with these professorial, peer, and cult challenges is to commit publicly to your own faith. My own children and many of my former students actually strengthened their faith when put on the defensive. Forced to reconsider more deeply their Catholic tradition, they became more active practitioners of faith than ever before.

However, it is important to remember that you cannot practice your religion alone. You will need a support group to help you maintain your religious identity. In fact, the biggest threat to keeping the faith comes from within yourself, rather than from professors, other students, or cults. With your newfound freedom, you will be under tremendous pressure to adopt the attitudes of your peers, especially in the areas of sex, drinking, and drugs. Always remember, though, that freedom from external restraints like parents always looking over your shoulder does not magically make right something that is inherently wrong.

Your first week at college, make it a top priority to contact the campus ministry office, whether you are at a state, private, or Catholic university. Campus ministry is a vital part of the church's outreach to help you develop a mature, adult faith. It is often one of the most vital organizations on campus. Its main goals are to help you belong to a vibrant faith community that helps you to develop religiously and to be a justice-loving member of Christ's body.

For Catholics, campus ministry at many state and private colleges takes the form of a Newman Club, a time-honored organization on college campuses. Newman Clubs sponsor many socials as well as religious functions like weekly Mass, retreats, spiritual direction, service projects, and study groups. They are a good place to meet like-minded students who are serious about their faith but also want to share fun times together.

Service

Douglas Coupland, the coiner of the term "Generation X" (those born between 1961 and 1980), has the narrator of his novel *Life After God* conclude his spiritual quest this way:

My secret is that I need God—that I am sick and can no longer make it alone. I need God to help me give, because I no longer seem to be capable of giving; to help me be kind, as I no longer seem capable of kindness; to help me love, as I seem beyond being able to love.[8]

After a long introspective look into his life and those of his friends, Coupland's hero discovered that there exists a powerful link between faith in God and the power to love, in giving, and in serving others. He is right.

A dynamic faith, sustained by a caring and loving community and nourished by prayer and worship, will eventually manifest itself in some kind of loving service of others.

Plan to make service a part of your college experience. Perhaps you'll want to volunteer at a hospital like my daughter did. Maybe you will help at a local food bank or travel to Appalachia during spring break with other college students to rehabilitate depressed housing units. Or possibly you and some college friends will work for Habitat for Humanity, an organization that constructs houses for the poor, in an area near your campus. The opportunities to serve are many. Check with your campus ministry office or student life center to find various projects that are seeking volunteers.

Service has many benefits. You will grow in love and strengthen your relationship with Jesus who said: "In so far as you did this to one of the least of these brothers of mine, you did it to me" (Mt 25:40). Your faith will be authentic because it is active, committed to doing justice. And through volunteer work, you might even find your niche in life and open new career opportunities. For example, I became a teacher because of my volunteer work as a catechism teacher and at an orphanage where I taught swimming and first aid.

Finally, service will help you cope with the stresses of college life. After a lecture on mental health, the famous psychiatrist Karl Menninger was asked, "What would you tell a person who felt a nervous breakdown coming on?"

Menninger replied, contrary to his audience's expectations,

"Lock up your house, go across the railway tracks, find someone in need, and then do something to help the person."

If you serve others, you will find more abundant life.

Witness

There are three kinds of people: those who make things happen, those who watch things happen, and those who don't know what is happening. Undoubtedly, you will want to be the first type, a take-charge college student who glorifies God by seeing God's presence in everything and who will use your many gifts to grow into a mature, intelligent Christian thinker.

A terrific way to maintain your Christian identity in college is simply to commit yourself to a pursuit of truth. Regardless of your course of study, when you develop your mind and hone your thinking skills, you are on a quest for Jesus who is the foundation of truth. Committing yourself to academic excellence will make you stand out. Furthermore, a discerning mind will enable you to unmask the shoddiness of today's culture and recognize the demons that promote false values like relativism and a secularism that deifies human cleverness.

With a keen mind, you can witness to your faith by defending truth, by challenging prejudicial statements against the faith, and by questioning assumptions that unthinkingly accept the conventional morality of the day. College will present many other opportunities to proclaim your faith—informal rap sessions with classmates, papers you write for philosophy and other classes, conversations with your roommate. Sharing your faith with others will strengthen it and may even help lead others to embrace it.

What if you feel unprepared to explain your faith, perhaps due to an inadequate religious education? Here's the advice I have offered my own students and children: You can take a theology course from a faith-filled Catholic professor, join a campus ministry study group, keep handy a copy of a Catholic catechism, and read some good introductory theology books on your religion. Adopt these and other ideas to help you grow in knowledge of your religion so you can witness it to others.

Conclusion

I want to thank you for reading this book. I hope some of the tips will help make your first few months at college a little easier. Congratulations again on beginning this exciting part of your life's journey. I will keep you in my prayers. I hope God will continue to bless you with much wisdom and love.

Yours in Christ,

Michael F. Pennock

Notes

One
1. "Catholic Higher Education: What Happened?—A Parent's Lament," *Commonweal*, April 9, 1993, p. 15.
2. Anthony De Mello, S.J., *Awareness* (New York: Doubleday, 1990), p. 76.

Two
1. *It Was on Fire When I Lay Down on It* (New York: Ivy Books, Ballantine, 1989), pp. 78-79.
2. Barry Guinah, "Homesickness in the Freshman Year," *Journal of the Freshman Year Experience*, November 1, 1992: pp. 111-120. The study also discovered that females experience homesickness more than males.
3. If you want to read his other rules to live by, see Robert Fulghum, *All I Really Need to Know I Learned in Kindergarten* (New York: Ivy Books, 1988), pp. 4-5.

Three
1. This really happened to a student who tells her story in *Reader's Digest*, October 1995, p. 113.

Four
1. Jack Canfield and Mark Victor Hansen, *A Second Helping of Chicken Soup for the Soul* (Deerfield Beach, Fl: Health Communications, Inc., 1995), p. 174. You will enjoy sipping from this and the other *Chicken Soup* books. They contain some great stories to inspire and encourage.
2. Christopher F. Monte, *Merlin: The Sorcerers' Guide to Survival in College* (Belmont, CA: Wadsworth Publishing Co., 1990), pp. 23-49.
3. *Glamour*, October 1995, p. 100.
4. Charles Shelton, Ph.D., reports these last three examples in his book *Pastoral Counseling with Adolescents and Young Adults* (New York: Crossroad, 1995), pp. 153, 167, 177.
5. Henry Wechsler, "Health and Behavioral Consequences of Binge Drinking in College: A National Survey of Students at 140 Campuses," *JAMA, The Journal of American Medical Association*, December 7, 1994, p. 1672 (6).
6. *The New York Times*, April 6, 1995, p. A11, A21.
7. Colman McCarthy, "Drinking, Learning Don't Mix at College," *National Catholic Reporter*, November 3, 1995, p. 18.
8. *The Chronicle of Higher Education*, July 14, 1993, B1-2.
9. See Daniel R. Levine's interesting article, "Cheating in Our Schools: A National Scandal," in *Reader's Digest*, October, 1995, pp. 65-70.
10. See Levine, pp. 66-67

Five
1. Teresa Tritch, "Give a College This Safety Test—Evaluating the Crime on College Campuses," *Money*, Winter 1994, pp. 32 ff.
2. See Ted J. Rakstis, "A Life's Deathwish: Suicide on Campus," *Circle K*, November/December 1989, pp. 10-13.
3. See Michael J. Hunt, C.S.P., *College Catholics: A New Counter-Culture* (New York: Paulist Press, 1993), pp. 98-99. This is a hopeful book by a long-time chaplain at Tufts University and other campuses.
4. Bobby Jindal, "Ivy League Catholicism," *Crisis*, September 1992, p. 35.
5. Arthur Jones, "Campus Ministry Fills Need as Funds Shrink," *National Catholic Reporter in America Online*, March 15, 1996, p. 1.
6. Michael J. Hunt, "Catholic Identity Goes to College," *The Catholic World*, May-June 1994, pp. 124ff.
7. Michael J. Buckley, "The Catholic University and Its Inherent Promise," *America*, May 1993, p. 14.
8. Douglas Coupland, *Life After God* (New York: Pocket Books, 1994), p. 359.